Richard Stephens

and the Clevedon

Motor Cars

To Michael
With Best Wish[es]
from
Bill

*Robin Loder Driving the Prototype Stevens Car and
Richard Eastmead Driving the 1900 Hackney Carriage
in the 1995 Evelyn Ellis Centenary Run*

Richard Stephens

and the Clevedon

Motor Cars

The Life and Work
of

Richard Stephens

Professor William Fairney
FREng FEng FIET

3

PUBLISHED IN THE UNITED KINGDOM BY:

Diesel Publishing
2, The Tithe Barn
High Street
Hawkesbury Upton
Badminton
South Gloucestershire GL9 1AY

www. fairdiesel.co.uk

British Library Cataloguing in Publication Data.
A catalogue record for this book is available from the British Library.

ISBN 978-0-9554455-4-5

Design by William Fairney

Edited by Pamela Smith

Printed and bound by Ta Kung Printing, Shenzhen, China

4

Contents

Foreword

When, as a youth of 16, I joined the Veteran Car Club in 1961, the then President was Richard Stephens. I met and talked to him on a number of occasions and although in the tale that follows he features as 'Dick', I knew him as Mr Stephens, and I only ever called him 'Sir'! He was immensely proud of the prototype Stephens motorcar, built by his father Richard Stephens Senior, on which as a boy he had learnt to drive before the 19th century had expired, and he still enjoyed using it on suitable occasions. For a Victorian motorcar it always seemed to go exceedingly well and I recall how on the 1963 International Rally it arrived at the checkpoint I was manning at the top of Bury Hill in the Sussex Downs. Both driver and car were completely untroubled by a climb that had seen quite a number of the Veterans 'tacking' across the gradient to lessen its severity.

In 1989 I became editor of *The Automobile,* an old car magazine, and one of the first tasks that I set myself was to make a list of car makes that had received little or scant attention from motoring writers. The Stephens was there, but although we shone the light on many neglected makes during my three-year stint in the editor's chair, I was unable to find a contributor who would tackle the make and I never found time to deal with the task myself. Until now, the story Richard Stephens Snr, a British pioneer-builder of motorcars in the unlikely location of the seaside resort of Clevedon in Somerset, has never been adequately told.

I am therefore delighted that Bill Fairney has taken on the responsibility to research and narrate, not only the story of the Stephens motorcars and their fascinating technicalities, but also to describe the personalities involved and historical context within which the cars were built. His interest in Stephens was whetted when researching his book *The Knife and Fork Man,* that records the work and life of the engineer Charles Redrup, who worked with Stephens at the turn-of-the-century.

As a result of Bill Fairney's labours we now have a book that will satisfy not only those who appreciate history in general terms, but also motoring historians who like to know the details about the motor vehicles that form the core of their interest.

Malcolm Jeal
Chairman of the Society of Automotive Historians in Britain

June 2009

Acknowledgements

I first became aware of the remarkable work of Richard Stephens whilst researching an earlier book about the life of Charles Redrup, who married Stephens' niece. Charles Redrup was an engineer who was recruited by Richard Stephens to chauffeur his cars and to act as a development and after-sales engineer.

I was soon made aware that two Stephens cars were still in existence and their owner Robin Loder was good enough to let me inspect them. I am most grateful to Robin for the time he spent with me and for the mass of information which he has provided about the cars.

It was through Robin that I learnt that Richard Stephens' grand-daughter Georgina Westlake had some information about the family. When I contacted Georgina she most generously invited me to visit her and view her scrapbook which proved to be a major archive of photographs, documents and artefacts about her grandfather and his cars. Georgina allowed me to copy the material I needed for the Redrup biography but I remained aware that there was much more to tell.

The Clevedon Civic Society had reprinted a brochure, *Clevedon Past* which contained a brief summary of Stephens' achievements and the members of the Society gave me further information. After the Redrup book *The Knife and Fork Man* was published I was invited to give a talk to the Civic Society, which I did in early 2008. At the meeting the Chairman Rob Campbell light-heartedly said "Why not do the Richard Stephens story next?" I replied that I thought it was a possibility but that there might not be enough material. How wrong I was!

In February 2009 Rob rang me and asked "How's the book coming on?" Not having done anything significant to progress it, I muttered "Slowly, slowly!" However Rob's call was sufficient to spur me into action and over the next few weeks I undertook the research.

The members of the Civic Society have been a tremendous help in providing material. Alan Blackmore provided me with several references from the *Clevedon Mercury,* whilst Jane Lilley supplied numerous quotations and references from local minutes and other records as well as photographs from her extensive collection. Rob Campbell has equally provided information and anecdotes as well as archive material from Arch Binding's service history.

Malcolm Jeal, Chairman of the Society of Automotive Historians in Britain, as well as writing an authoritative Foreword, kept me on the straight and narrow, not only on historical accuracy, but also by virtually proof-reading the book as he did so. He also supplied the photographs for the Frontispiece and those of Gough's Cave and of the 1896 Emancipation Run.

Julia Elton, President of the Clevedon Civic Society gave generously of her time to enable me to research the Elton archives, from which much valuable original source material has resulted, including the photographs which I was able to take of the prototype gas lighters. Julia also pointed me in the direction of the DVD of the 2006 Cavalcade of veteran and vintage cars, and to Roger Triggol whose background knowledge of the Stephens and of other veteran cars was invaluable.

Sid and Audrey Marks are great cycling enthusiasts and kept me entranced by their archives of cycling photographs and memorabilia. I am particularly indebted to them for information about ladies' dress clips and for the photographs of their collection.

Mrs Joan Redrup was again kind enough to let me draw on the Charles Benjamin Redrup archives for the section about him. These Archives are now lodged with the Manchester Museum of Science and Industry together with the collection of Redrup engines. I am grateful to the Aerospace Curator Mr Nick Forder for assistance in making this happen.

I have endeavoured to locate the copyright owners of the photographs and seek their permission but have not always been successful. To those I have been able to contact, and to all whom I have not been able to mention, many thanks.

When I contacted Georgina Westlake once more to tell her that I was to write the book about her grandfather she immediately invited me to visit her again to delve into the Stephens archives. Having previously only touched the surface of these records I was amazed to find so much more information about the Clevedon years and also previously unseen brochures and information about the Stephens family after they moved to London. Without Georgina's help this book would have been just a shadow of its present form.

Many thanks are due to Pamela Smith who not only proofed and edited the book, but is a friend of many years' standing.

Finally my thanks go to my wife Linda, who has supplied me with gallons of coffee, other sustenance and great support over the last three hectic months of writing.

William Fairney
Hawkesbury |Upton
May 2009

Chapter 1
The Early Years

The latter half of the nineteenth century was a time of rapid change and the Industrial Revolution was in full swing. With the development of the steam engine and the invention of industrial electric motors, productivity in farming, manufacture, mining and steel production was rising rapidly. It was a time for entrepreneurs everywhere to exploit their talents in harnessing these new technologies.

Richard Stephens was born in Cwmbran near Pontypool in South Wales in 1856 and like many in that part of Wales went down the coal mines as a very young man. His family originated in mid-Wales but his father, Edward Stephens, moved to Cwmbran to obtain work in the mines.

Edward Stephens was from what was then Radnorshire, born in 1796 in the village of Llanbadarnfyndd. He worked as an agricultural labourer and married his first wife Mary Harding in 1832. Mary was the same age as Edward and came from Abbeycwmhir. By 1841 they had two children, Edward, 6 and Ann, 3 and were living in Dufferin Cottage, Knighton, Radnor. According to the 1851 census Mary was still living at this address with her daughter Ann, but Edward was now living in Cwmbran with the lady who was to become his second wife, Margaret.

It is not known why Edward moved to Cwmbran; perhaps the agricultural industry was going through one of its regular slumps. More likely however, is that Edward had heard about the wages to be earned in South Wales, because it appears he went to work in the coal and iron ore mining industry, for which the town was well known. The mining of ore dates back to the Iron and Bronze Ages and it is known that the Romans had to overcome the Silurian Tribe to take possession of the rich resources. In the eighteenth century a canal link to the Newport docks enabled a strong industry to develop, with the local limestone also being used for smelting and cement-making.

The invention of the coking process resulted in the development of a steel industry in the nineteenth century, because coke was purged of the impurities, particularly sulphur, which in coal caused iron to be too brittle when smelted. The establishment of foundries and the blast furnace enabled the steel-making industry to grow rapidly. Tin mining and smelting was also established. This continued well into the twentieth century until the depression of the 1920s led to massive unemployment and decimation of the industry.

However in the 1860s the industry was flourishing and Edward would have had little difficulty in finding work. By 1861, when Margaret was still just 33, they were married with five children, the first born in 1849. Of these Richard Stephens, the subject of this book, was born in Cwmbran on 8th May 1856. He had three brothers, John, born in 1849, David, (Davey), born in 1851 and Morris, born in 1854. His sister, Cecilia, was born in 1859. He also had his half-sister Ann and several half brothers.

Edward, who was already suffering from emphysema, was involved in a mine explosion in November 1863 and suffered a broken thigh. He contracted a chest infection and died six weeks later leaving Margaret to bring up a family ranging in age from four to fourteen. It is not surprising then that the young boys also went to work in the South Wales coalmines.

Nothing is known about what education they received, but Richard entered the pits at the age of seven. He was industrious and intelligent and by his teens he had been made an engine driver at the Little Pit at Nantyglo, part of the Nantyglo and Blaina Ironworks Co. Ltd. He also joined the mine's brass band and learnt to play the trumpet. His training took him to other mining areas and in 1871 he was playing as a visiting Band Boy in St Germans, Cornwall.

Steam engines were by this time in wide use in mining. Static engines were used for both pumping out water and raising cages of men or coal to the surface. Traction engines were used for hauling wagons of coal or iron ore or limestone from the pit shaft to the storage areas and for despatch onto the rail network.

The earliest recorded steam engine dates back to the first century AD when Hero of Alexandria mounted a sphere on an axle and partly-filled it with water. Two diametrically opposite spouts emitted steam when the sphere was heated over a fire. The spouts were bent so that the reaction of the steam rotated the sphere about the axle. However the Aeolipile as it was called, did not drive anything. (Plate 1.1).

It is interesting to note that this engine not only preceded the reciprocating steam engine by nearly two millenia but was the first turbine reaction engine. The first recorded design for a steam impulse engine also pre-dates Charles A Parsons, the inventor of the modern steam turbine. In the published works of Taqi al-Din in 1551, he described a bladed wheel driven by steam from a boiling kettle, coupled to a spit over a fire, for cooking meat. (Plate 1.2). Apparently James

Plate 1.1   Hero's   Aeolipile

Watt was not the first to observe boiling kettles!

A more practical application was described in 1629 by Giovanni Branca. His drawing shows a pitcher of boiling water spurting steam onto a vaned wheel. In his text he states that it might be used for powering pestles and mortars, grinding machines, raising water, and sawing wood. (Plate 1.3).

The first practical steam-powered engine used in a mine was a water pump, developed in 1698 by Thomas Savery who was an English military engineer and inventor. He got the idea from the pressure cooker invented in 1679 by the French mathematician and physicist Denis Papin. Because it used an atmospheric lift pump its lifting capability

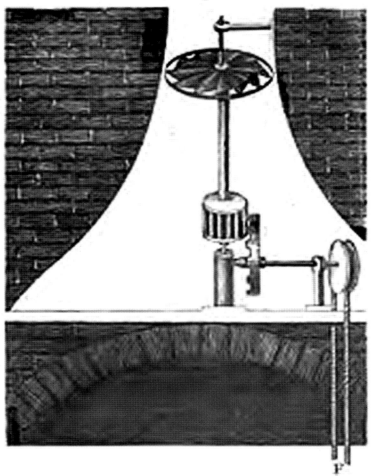

Plate 1.2   Taqi al-Din's Impulse Turbine

was restricted to about thirty-two feet (9.8m). It was also prone to boiler explosions.

Newcomen's atmospheric engine, invented around 1710, paved the way for the Industrial Revolution. It was relatively inefficient, and in most cases was only used for pumping water, being employed to drain mine workings at previously impossible depths. It was also used for providing a recycled flow of water for factory water wheels where a local water supply was not available. (Plate 1.4).

It was James Watt however who transformed Newcomen's primitive steam engine into a truly practical motive power for industry. As a twelve-year old boy Watt was observed by his mother to watch a boiling

Plate 1.3   *Branca's Turbine*

Plate 1.4   *Early Newcomen Steam Engine*

14

kettle for hours on end. James noted how the steam, unable to escape soley from the spout, bubbled its way around the lid, pushing it up as it did so. He also noted that when he partially blocked the spout with a teaspoon, the lid would stay partly raised as the steam escaped. Tradition says that it was from these observations that Watt recognised the power of steam and went on to design his engine.

But the power of steam was already well known. The more probable explanation is that Watt realised that there was a self-stabilising process at play whereby the internal pressure was just balanced by the weight of the lid. He was discovering the concept of stabilising negative feedback, which was to figure in his invention of the steam governor, many years later.

Watt analysed Newcomen's engine and discovered that most of the heat energy was wasted on heating the cylinder for each cycle. The engine worked by passing low-grade steam into the cylinder then injecting cold water to condense the steam. Atmospheric pressure then pushed the piston down. For the next cycle, most of the heat in the steam went to heating the cylinder again.

Watt turned the process upside down. He used the steam pressure to force the piston down, then exhausted the used steam to an external condensing vessel. He made this process efficient by fitting air pumps to the condenser to reduce the air pressure inside it to suck the steam out. By keeping the cylinder hot, and insulating it with a jacket, he was able to reduce the heat losses from the system, raise the working temperature and so improve the efficiency of the engine by a factor of four.

Early steam engines were beam engines as in Plate 1.4, in which one end of a horizontal beam was moved up and down by the steam-driven piston. The other end of the beam drove the piston of a water pump. Watt devised a crank system to change the reciprocating motion into rotational motion making the engine suitable for a wide range of industrial applications. Incorporation of a boiler safety valve and of a speed governor completed the basic concept which has stood the test of time.

The first recorded use of a steam engine to drive a self-propelled vehicle is that of French engineer Nicolas Cugnot. His self-propelled three-wheeled vehicle, developed primarily for towing artillery, was demonstrated on 23rd October 1769 in the Paris arsenal, but his second engine had an unfortunate accident and was written off, as was Cugnot's venture into steam transport.

Richard Trevithick of Cornwall developed steam engines for mines using high pressure steam and made a road-running traction engine

Plate 1.5 Trevithick Locomotive

in about 1800. The first use of a steam engine for a railway was in South Wales near Merthyr Tydfil with the train running between the villages of Penydarren and Abercynon. Trevithick had been experimenting with his locomotive for some months, but had hitherto been running it on the ground. The track on which he ran the locomotive had long been in place as a horse-drawn tramway before the experiment.

Its purpose had been the transport of iron from the foundries of the Penydarren-Dowlais area to the Glamorganshire Canal at Abercynon. (Plate 1.5). On the initial run, the train carried seventy men and ten tons of iron. It covered the 9½ miles to Abercynon in slightly over two hours. The concept was proved. However, the technology was not trouble-free. Not the engine, but the rails proved to be the problem. The iron rails used for the track were brittle and the massive weight of the locomotive plus its heavy load soon resulted in fractured rails. The solution lay in the nearby ironworks, but it was some years before high quality resilient steel rails were available at an economic rate.

Nantyglo is near the head of the Ebbw Fach river to the south of Brynmawr, which is the highest town in South Wales. Nantyglo means 'Stream of Coal'. It lived up to its name and it was a combined coal mine and ironworks. The enterprise started in 1789 when the Earl of Abergavenny leased the land to a group of industrialists. The ironworks were built in 1795, and within the year there were two furnaces, several forges, a steam engine and necessary buildings and machinery for smelting and forging iron ore. The work force came from all over Great Britain and at its peak employed over 3,000 people. The works had a chequered history as demand for iron and coal rose and fell but it benefited from the use of coke using the open-hearth process. The two seams of the Nantyglo pit produced excellent steam coal for local use and export to surrounding counties and overseas. (Plate 1.6).

In 1844 the large Lion Mill with blast furnaces for refining steel was built and Nantyglo became famous worldwide for the quality of its product. The seven blast furnaces produced over 70,000 tons of steel a year for export and home consumption. Living conditions for the workers were poor and they were forced under the Truck system to buy their goods from the Company, often at artificially high prices. This iniquitous system virtually enslaved the workers who had no alternative employment opportunities and who frequently fell into debt which kept them in poverty. Periodic falls in the price of iron led to falls in wages, leading to further extremes of poverty and to occasional unrest. Riots in 1816 and 1822 had been quelled by a mixture of negotiation and

Plate 1.6   Nantyglo Coal Mine and Iron Works

threatened force but the Company owners felt sufficiently at risk to build two castles, or 'round towers' as they were called, to retire to in the event of further riots.

The works were served by rail links to the Great Western and the London and North Western Railways. Limestone for smelting came by a third railway from quarries at Llangattock. The yards themselves were served by over three hundred miles of tramways above and below ground. It was not surprising then that Richard Stephens found employment on the Nantyglo railways. He had a natural aptitude for mechanical engineering and soon became expert in operating and maintaining these engines. This training was to stand him in good stead for his later career.

The mine-owners, recognising Richard's abilities, gave him training in hard-rock mining. Part of his training took him to other locations; Cornwall, where he learnt about rock and excavation; caves in the Mendips where he learnt about geology and rock formations. He became a hard rock driller, which requires great expertise and skill. As drilling progresses and different kinds of rock are encountered the choice of drill head is crucial. Soft rocks such as shale require a boring force of just a few tons per square inch, and a soft drill head. If hard rock is suddenly found this drill head can break off and jam the borehole.

18

Plate 1.7   John and Elizabeth Stacey and Daughter Jessie

Very hard rock requires boring forces of up to fifty tons per square inches and diamond cutters. The diamonds have to be set in the drill head with great accuracy otherwise eccentric cutting occurs and diamonds may break off. Whilst industrial-grade diamonds are far cheaper than jewellery-grade, they are still very valuable and an obvious target for rough and ready miners seeking their fortune. The diamond-setter therefore has to be a man of great integrity and able to choose and manage reliable drill crews.

Whilst working in the mines Richard made a number of new acquaintances, including an expert in deep mining, John Stacey, (Plate 1.7), who had travelled extensively overseas as a consultant. In 1877 Stacey became engaged to a farm labourer's seventeen year-old daughter, Elizabeth Masters, from Pilton, near Shepton Mallet. The second eldest daughter, Mary Ann Masters, soon came to the attention of Richard Stephens and they became engaged in the same year

William and Sarah Masters had a family of three sons and three daughters, the eldest being Elizabeth. The father William had a brother George and he and his wife, also Elizabeth, lived in Clevedon, Somerset. They had a son, also George, who was born with a hump back. George senior died young and Elizabeth, a dressmaker, was left to bring up her son alone.

Clevedon was the seat of the Elton family who lived in Clevedon Court, a stately home with roots back to the thirteenth century. The Seventh Baronet, Sir Arthur Elton was a great benefactor of the town and very progressive, developing gas and water works of the highest standard. His son and heir to the Baronetcy was Edmund Harry Elton, who lived at a family home, Firwood, near to the estate. He was a keen inventor and amateur potter. The plight of Elizabeth and George came to his attention and he took George straight from school and trained him as a gardener and as a potter.

The Nantyglo and Blaina Ironworks Co. Ltd. continued to trade but became increasingly financially unviable and ultimately in March 1874 the Nantyglo works closed. In order to meet the pressing demands of their creditors the whole of the machinery, engines, railways etc. and every bit of iron that could be found was scavenged and sold.

By 1878 the works were entirely dismantled and only the dilapidated buildings left standing. It is likely that Richard was involved in this dismantling process for he embarked on his next venture during 1877. The coal and steel industry in Britain was going through one of its periodic slumps, but Richard had to secure employment somewhere. Armed with his set of skills as engine driver and hard rock driller, he looked around for further employment.

John Stacey introduced Richard to a number of his friends and Richard then embarked on the first of a number of international ventures. He obtained a contract in Australia and set sail in 1877. He joined a mining company in New South Wales and started work as a driller. In addition he worked as a blacksmith in his spare time to save money for his forthcoming marriage. In the following year he sent for Mary and

Plate 2.1   Thomas Edison and an early Phonograph

Whilst Humphry Davy had demonstrated a crude carbon arc lamp as early as 1800, it was Joseph Swan who made the first carbon filament lamps between 1850 and 1860. He returned to the problem in 1875 when better vacuum pumps became available and in Newcastle, England in 1878 he publicly demonstrated a carbon-filament lamp. Thomas Edison, hearing of this success, made carbon filament lamps in 1879 in which the filament was of bamboo. His engineers at Menlo Park soon improved on this and Edison set up several companies to promote the new technology.

The first commercial electric light system was installed on Pearl Street in Lower Manhattan in 1882, but even earlier, the lighting system was taken abroad to the Paris Lighting Exposition in 1881, the Crystal Palace in London in 1882 and the coronation of the Czar in Moscow. The development of electric lighting led Edison to invest in the business of electricity generation and distribution. In this his judgement failed him, for he backed the Direct Current system which was soon to succumb to Alternating Current generation after Steinmetz invented the now ubiquitous induction motor.

In 1881 Edison formed the Edison Ore-Milling Co. to industrialise his process for extracting various metals from ore. The iron ore mines in New Jersey around where Edison lived had become depleted and only low-grade ore remained. Edison's new process would take low-grade ore, crush it and separate out the iron using magnetic separators. The first installation was at the Ogden mine in Sparta, Sussex County. The Ogden works had been in operation since 1772, producing high-grade magnetite ore of superior quality and it was smelted in furnaces in nearby Hopewell and Franklin. Of late, the quality had declined and the mine had virtually stopped production since 1873. The great vein of lower-grade ore was two miles long and of unknown depth. The Edison process was the only hope for rescuing the mine.

Edison visited the construction site regularly and his brother oversaw the project. However it did not survive the fiercely competitive world of steel-making. The cost of power to drive the huge magnetic separators meant that the cost of the concentrated ore was still higher than the cost of high-grade ore imported from other sites and the enterprise failed. By 1887 Edison had developed the process further and taken out new patents. He formed in 1889, the New Jersey and Pennsylvania Concentrating Works and became deeply absorbed in the project. He began to spend much time away from home at the mines in Ogdensburg, New Jersey and at the new plant in Humboldt where the low-grade ore was still sufficiently high in magnetite to make the project appear viable. The Cleveland Iron Cliffs had heard about the new process and thought it would be a way to revive the fortunes of the Humboldt mine and so commissioned Edison to build them a magnetic separator plant.

According to family legend Richard Stephens broke his journey to Humboldt to spend some time in Lansing, Michigan, to see an interesting steam-driven vehicle, probably that which had been developed in that year by an ingenious engineer Ransom Eli Olds. (Plate 2.2).

In 1885 Olds was making industrial steam engines with his father, Pliny Fisk Olds, who owned a small machine shop. In that year Ransom also started experimenting with gasoline burners for raising steam in the boilers. By 1887 he had fitted a steam engine to a three-wheeled carriage, but it was very underpowered. Richard Stephens is reputed to have worked with Olds, helping him develop the steam engine and the burners, but Richard was most interested in the gasoline burners. He thought out some ideas of his own in which the burners would be placed directly inside the cylinders as Benz had done with his gasoline engine. He and Olds drafted layouts for such an engine. However as Richard's contract at the Humboldt mine was due to start soon, he reluctantly took his leave of Olds for the time being.

Plate 2.2   Ransom Eli Olds

Edison's Project Manager at Humboldt was one of his inventors from Menlo Park, an ex-patriate Englishman William Kennedy Laurie Dickson. Richard Stephens became involved in the project and got to know Dickson well. He also met Thomas Edison on his regular visits to the plant and spent time with him discussing Edison's work and his own ideas for future development of gasoline engines.

Edison was facing competition with his Phonograph from some rival inventors who had patented the use of wax cylinders. He was using all his ingenuity to get around the patents but it distracted him from his other projects so he set up a new company and engaged staff to licence out the latest machine for demonstrations.

Edison's English agent was Colonel George Gouraud, a veteran of the American Civil War and a holder of the Congressional Medal of Honour. Gouraud had established an office in his home in London, named after Edison's Menlo works. It was called Little Menlo, and located on Beulah Hill in Upper Norwood. He converted it to be an advertisement for the Edison Company, equipping it with the latest electrical appliances and holding dinner parties for the most exalted in the land. He was selling Edison telephone and telegraphic machines but was aware that Edison was close to perfecting the Phonograph. He sailed to America in May 1888 and returned in June with a number of Phonographs and proceeded to demonstrate them in London.

On 29th June recordings were made of a Handel concert at Crystal Palace, and Gouraud proceeded to make recordings of a number of speeches and readings by public figures. A notable recording after a dinner at Little Menlo was of the composer Arthur Sullivan (later Sir Arthur). In it Sullivan toasts Edison and his new machine, saying that it both astonished and terrified him. He was astonished to think that marvellous music could be recorded for posterity, but terrified that horrible music would also be preserved. How right he was!

Later in 1888 Edison, still distracted from his other projects, sold his Phonograph companies to an astute businessman Jesse Lippincott who had bought the rival wax cylinder patents and eventually persuaded Edison to join with him. Edison eventually tired of the project and sold the US rights to Lippincott who marketed the machine for sale and for hire. In America at this time Richard Stephens bought one of these Phonographs from Lippincott.

Whilst at Humboldt, Richard and Mary received some tragic news. Mary's brother-in-law John Stacey was still involved in deep mining and in 1888 he was offered the position as a consultant to a South African diamond mining company. Leaving his family of Elizabeth and three daughters behind in Swansea, he went to South Africa to take up his engagement. Unfortunately he had only been there a short time when he caught yellow fever. The prognosis at that time was very poor and Stacey soon succumbed to the disease. Elizabeth was left to bring up her three daughters on her own.

With Richard's work at the Humbold plant virtually at an end, and Mary's health in poor condition, he tidied up his affairs and the family left for home in early 1889. Through Mary's cousin George, working for Sir Edmund Elton who had succeeded to the Baronetcy in 1883 when his father Sir Arthur died, Richard had heard of a part-time post in the small Somerset town of Clevedon, which would give him time to develop some ideas of his own.

On his way home Richard may have called in to see Ransom Olds again in Lansing to see what progress Olds was making with the steam car and his progress towards a gasoline engine. Later, in 1892, Olds tested a two-cylinder steam car. (Plate 2.3). In August 1897 he established the Olds Motor Vehicle Company with the first of a long line of Oldsmobile cars being sold in 1901.

Plate 2.3   Olds Steam Car 1892

The Humboldt separator plant proved a failure. It could not produce ore of high enough grade or in sufficient quantities to make the project economically viable. The ore also contained high levels of phosphorus which was a major problem in smelting. Edison's process did not succeed in removing it. In December 1890 the mill was destroyed by a major fire and the project failed.

Richard Stephens and his family returned to the United Kingdom in early 1889 to Clevedon. Richard took with him the Phonograph which he had obtained from Jesse Lippincott who had purchased the rights to the phonograph from Edison. He sold Richard the rights to use and hire it out in the United Kingdom. However Lippincott became ill in 1890 and was unable to attend to the business which fell into debt. Edison bought back the companies but did not have the time to operate them as a hire business and decided to concentrate on outright sales. This later led to some difficulties for Richard because Lippincott's rights to the hiring out of the machines did not extend beyond the USA and Canada.

Richard's brother Davey went home to South Wales at the same time that Richard and Mary returned. He married a girl from Barry, where they settled in the village of Briton Ferry. Eventually they moved to the USA and became naturalised citizens but proved useful contacts for Richard with America.

Clevedon at the turn of the twentieth century was a mixture of seaside resort for the gentility and a retirement refuge for the wealthy. The Mendip Hills extend in a line across Somerset and meet the Bristol Channel at Clevedon and Weston-super-Mare. Located on the side of a cliff on the sunny northern coast of Somerset, Clevedon enjoys lovely views over the Channel. The warmth of the Gulf Stream combined in summer with warm south-westerly breezes makes it an ideal refuge for the retired and those recovering from illness. The residents would walk along the promenade and down the pier, or if incapacitated, would be pushed in their bath chairs by their families or retainers.

The graceful pier that extends into the Bristol Channel is considered to be the best preserved example of its architectural type. It has recently been restored to its full Victorian splendour, and has been listed Grade I by English Heritage. (Plate 2.4). Clevedon developed as a resort for Bristol from around 1795, but it was the arrival of a railway in 1847 that led to hopes for its rapid development. It was thought that a new pier would not only provide an addition to the resort but also a jetty to enable steamers to ferry passengers to South Wales.

There were formidable problems to be overcome, with a tidal range of 47ft (14.2 metres), the second highest in the world, and huge currents,

Plate 2.4   Clevedon Pier

but addressing them resulted in the pier's very slender and elegant style. When it was opened in 1869 the pier was 840 ft (255 metres) long, with a six-level landing stage at its end. From this pier a ferry ran to Briton Ferry near Barry on the mouth of the river Neath in South Wales, which was an obvious destination being only thirteen miles across the water.

Clevedon was and still is the seat of the Elton family who have resided in Clifton Court since 1709, when Sir Abraham Elton bought the property plus 1,128 acres of land. The Eltons stemmed from Herefordshire and the earliest reference is of a John Elton living at Hazle. Since that time the family has expanded and many branches of the family now exist. A doctor, Thomas Elton is recorded as having left Ledbury and moved to Bristol in 1608. However he did not prosper in Bristol and moved to Bath a few years later, where he died.

It was another branch of the Eltons, probably from Newent in Gloucestershire, that also moved to Bristol and this time they flourished. The Eltons became merchants and grew wealthy over the next two centuries, financing shipping expeditions and the tobacco trade. In the 18th century the first Abraham Elton was a vigorous entrepreneur, trading in wines, tobacco and establishing copper and lead works. He used Bristol coal and lead ores from the Mendips to supply Abraham Darby's brass works at Baptist Mills on the river Frome. Abraham Elton was knighted in 1683 and in 1708 he became Master of the Merchant Venturers in Bristol. His eldest son, Abraham II, followed in his footsteps as Master a few years later.

Clevedon Court was built in 1320 by Sir John de Clevedon. He incorporated two earlier structures dating from 1190 and 1280 respectively. The Court naturally underwent many changes over the centuries until Abraham Elton bought it, when it was in a serious state of dilapidation. Whilst his father was occupied in Bristol with commerce, Abraham II set about the renovations. Successive generations of Eltons have seen their fortunes rise and fall but always Clevedon Court survived and remained the family seat, being visited by many worthies. William Makepeace Thackeray visited in October 1848 and several times subsequently, as he found inspiration for several of his works from the old manor, and also from one of the Elton ladies. Alfred Tennyson also called with his new wife in June 1850 whilst on a country tour.

The 7th Baronet, Sir Arthur Hallam Elton succeeded to the title in 1853, although he had been managing the estate for his father for the previous ten years. Trained at Sandhurst in surveying he had taken upon himself the task of further renovating Clevedon Court. (Colour Plate C3). He invested his immense energy in improving the water supply and drainage, not only on the estate but also in the surrounding villages. He established the Water Works Company and chaired the Board for the rest of his life. He had sewers built and promoted many building projects. He chaired the Board of the Pier Company and saw its construction through to completion. Clevedon had its own Gas Works by 1857 and although Sir Arthur sat on the Board, the town did not actually get gas light until 1863.

In November 1882 disaster struck at Clevedon Court. A chimney fire in the Red Room led to a major conflagration. Although the estate staff rolled out hoses the water pressure was insufficient to make any impression on the flames. This was a sorry plight for the Chairman of the Water Works Company. The West Wing of the Court was completely destroyed and many valuable books lost. Although restoration work began immediately, the family retired to the East Wing to supervise. Whether the disaster took its toll on Sir Arthur is not clear but in the summer of 1883 he had a stroke and died shortly afterwards.

Sir Edmund Elton and his wife Dame Agnes succeeded to the Baronetcy, just two hundred years after the First Baronet had taken the title. They had been living nearby at Firwood and were already involved in the restoration of Clevedon Court. At the time of the fire the town did not even possess a fire engine. Following the fire Sir Edmund established the Fire Brigade in the town and he himself became a keen fireman and could be seen assisting them whenever the need arose.

The Clevedon Borough Council had decided in late 1882 to purchase a steam-roller to help maintain the roads. This aroused some controversy as the town did not have a fire engine. It came to the notice of the London Fire Service and evoked a strong letter to the *Clevedon Mercury* from the editor of *The Fireman*, the professional journal:

It is simply ridiculous for any Authority to purchase a roller before a fire engine is of some valuable service in case of fire and can't be done without, whereas a steam roller can. I can scarcely think that any man would suggest such a thing in preference to a fire engine, especially after the recent fire at Clevedon Court. A fire engine would cost from £180 to £200, with all the necessary gear, whereas a steam roller would cost nearly three times the amount.

If a roller is required, why not get a hand one, drawn by horses, at a third of the cost? It is obvious that the authorities are not doing their duty to the Parish unless they avail themselves of the Local Government Act which enables them to borrow money to purchase such a fire engine.

Yours faithfully,

The Editor of *The Fireman*, Greenwich

Nevertheless the Council proceeded with the purchase of the steam roller and it was delivered on 2nd April 1883. The *Clevedon Mercury* also reported that an application had been accepted from a man to act as engineer to work the steam roller. He currently held a similar position with Littleborough Local Council. By June 1886 the work of rolling and stonebreaking had been suspended and the engine driver and foreman had been discharged, but in October of the same year the driver, a Mr Whitworth, had been re-engaged at thirty shillings a week. In September 1888 the driver had left and the post was re-advertised.

Sir Edmund Elton had many interests, one of which was pottery. Through Mary Stephens' cousin, George Masters. Sir Edmund knew of Richard Stephens and George had told him that Richard was an experienced traction-engine driver and was about to return home from the USA for family reasons. Sir Edmund suggested to George that he write to Richard, advising him of the steam-roller driver vacancy. Thus it was that the Stephens family found themselves in Clevedon, initially in Derbyshire Villas, Old Street and then at 6 Meadow Road.

Shortly after they were settled in Clevedon, in 1890, the family was visited by Mary's widowed sister Elizabeth Stacey and her three girls Jessie, Elizabeth and Rosa. As was often the practice in those days, Mary and Richard agreed to take over the upbringing of Jessie, the five-year old eldest daughter and so she lived with them and was raised in Clevedon. The other daughters lived in South Wales with Elizabeth but never lost contact with their sister.

Whilst in the United States Richard Stephens had seen developments in bicycle manufacture which made use of lightweight tubular steel frames. He therefore proposed to set himself up as a bicycle manufacturer and supplier preparatory to advancing his real ambition of making motor cars.

Richard intended to combine his job as steam roller driver, with this cycle business but first, he had to have some designs. He set about designing and attempting to patent various ideas he had picked up in the USA. He also started looking around for premises from which to operate whilst Mary sought some occupation to help bring in money for the family. The steam-roller driver's wage of twenty-eight shillings a week was a big drop from the diamond-setter's salary of seventy-five Canadian dollars a month.

In April 1889 Richard applied for a *Two-Wheeled Vehicles* patent No. 12061. However it seems likely that this lacked sufficient originality as it was either rejected or abandoned. In 1890 he tried again with application No. 6507 for *Two-wheeled Vehicles*, and No. 6743 for *Go-carts,* an early attempt at a car. However these too were rejected or abandoned. This did not stop him developing his designs for bicycles, but in the meantime he sold Starley safety bicycles.

James Starley of Coventry had invented the tangentially-spoked wheel and improved upon his *Ordinary Bicycle* in favour of the crank and chain design. His nephew John Starley invented the *Safety Bicycle* in which front and rear wheels are of equal size. Richard Stephens started by stocking the most up-to-date version then available, the Starley 'Swift' Bicycle. (Plate 2.5).

Some heavy snow during the winter of 1890/91 must have caused him problems with his road-roller work, for in January 1891, together with George William Knowles, he applied for a *Snow Ploughs for Footpaths, etc,* patent. This application was successful and was granted ion 1st January 1892. No doubt Richard had seen snow ploughs at work in the USA and Canada but this appears to be the first use in Britain.

Plate 2.5   A Starley Safety Bicycle

Richard and Mary's third son Arthur Ewart was born in August 1891, and Richard's quest for larger premises was eventually successful and so they moved to 112, Newbury Place on the Triangle in central Clevedon where the 1891 Census lists him as 'Traction Engine Driver and Machinist'. Here he started bicycle manufacture whilst Mary had sufficient space to set up a small tea shop to cater for the many visitors to Clevedon.

A notice over the premises declared:

The Clevedon Cycle Depot and Refreshment Rooms

In July 1891 Richard advertised in the *Clevedon Mercury:*

The best value in the market is the **'Swift Juvenile'**, £4.4s.
Stephens, machinist, repairs to cycles, sewing machines, lawnmowers
and all kinds of machinery;
Oil cans, alarm bells, lubricators, luggage carriers, lamps, saddles, handles etc.
Rubber tires for cycles, go-carts, perambulators, chairs etc, Silver-plating, enamelling, fittings, accessories etc. At trade prices

However Richard did not rely solely on the *Mercury* for his advertising. In 1893 he was admonished by the Local Board of Health for chalking advertisements on the decking of the pier! At that time he was probably promoting his wife's Refreshment Rooms or demonstrations of the Phonograph.

His *Mercury* advertisement appears to have brought some success for in March 1892 he received a contract from two brothers in Bristol, Thomas and George Ford, to manufacture seats for Bristol Tramways trams. These were to be:

a reversible-back, self-acting seat that will keep itself dry in wet weather ...... that each seat will be free from springs, cog wheels or other appliances liable to get out of order...

It is not known how many of these seats Richard manufactured but they were in service with the Bristol Tramways and Carriage Company for a very long time.

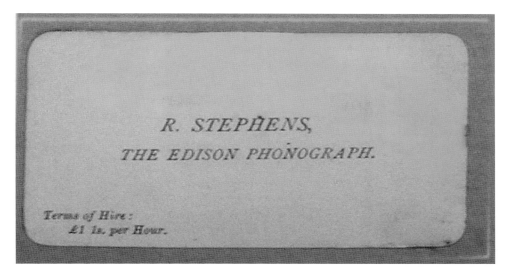

Plate 2.6   Stephens Travelling Phonograph Business Card

In June 1892 he tendered his resignation as steam roller driver so that he could devote more time to his engineering and cycle business. He also wanted to generate more income by demonstrating and hiring out his Phonograph. Whilst his cycle business was progressing well and he was developing the techniques required for car manufacture, his car designs were advancing and he needed to put more time into the development. Nevertheless he was prevailed upon by the town Board to reconsider and he offered to continue his duties for about another three weeks to finish the current work and to put the roller into good repair. He wanted a salary increase to thirty-three shillings a week instead of the current twenty-eight shillings but his offer was rejected and the Board asked him to continue at his present rate.

When Richard completed the work, nineteen year-old Edmund H Shopland, the son of an established Clevedon builder of Shopland Brothers, offered to take over at a weekly rate of twenty-six shillings, but The Board demurred and decided to advertise. By January 1893 no other offers were forthcoming so it was decided to give Shopland a trial. It was reported to the Board that Richard Stephens had resigned "as he had a better job travelling with a Phonograph." (Plate 2.6).

Richard had found that his earnings as a steam roller driver did not cover the costs of his bicycle and car development work. In 1891 a method of copying existing Phonograph recordings onto blank wax cylinders had become available from a rival of Edison. Stephens visited Colonel Gouraud at Little Menlo and purchased additional voice

41

recordings, but he also purchased a copying machine from Edison's rival. He travelled all over the country with the Phonograph and carried with him a number of recordings including some of speeches by Gladstone and Sir William Harcourt, the then Chancellor of the Exchequer.

He would hire out the Phonograph for one guinea per hour. He also had a limited number of blank wax cylinders with which he would make recordings of local celebrities. On a visit back to Nantyglo he recorded the voice of a young boy elocutionist, Ben Jelley, who had already won over fifty prizes at Eisteddfods. The record of a recitation of the poem *Rather Warm* was reproduced by Richard Stephens and sold widely at the time around the country. He also had recordings of poems recited by Lord Alfred Tennyson, of which the most famous is the 1890 recording of *The Charge of the Light Brigade.*

By 1894 Richard was selling bicycles of his own design, the *Clevedon Special*. (Plate 2.7). On August 18th 1894 the Clevedon Ameteur Athletics Association held their annual Sports Day at Clevedon Court. Richard's bicycle was shown prominently on the front page of the programme and sold for fifteen guineas. His business was described as *Engineer and Cycle Builder.*

In 1894 the Edison Company instituted legal proceedings against Lippincott and the people to whom he had granted licences outside of North America. The court case was long and protracted. Richard received a writ from the Edison-Bell Company in respect of royalties due. By October he had incurred such legal costs, and was so stretched by the development costs for his automobile design, that his creditors applied for a bankruptcy examination.

Richard explained to the Examiner at his hearing in November 1894 about his legal difficulties, saying that he had disposed of the phonograph to raise funds. He had paid the equivalent of seventy-five pounds for it but only received fifteen pounds when he sold it to a purchaser from Birmingham. His creditors were pushing for sale of all his possessions but Richard pleaded that his furniture could not be seized as his wife, who had her separate Refreshment Rooms business, had a claim on them.

The hearing was deferred for a month and in December he was declared bankrupt. Mary was allowed to keep their furniture so she could continue with the Refreshment Rooms. Richard applied for discharge from his bankruptcy in September 1897 and was released with final discharge deferred for five years. This does not appear to have affected

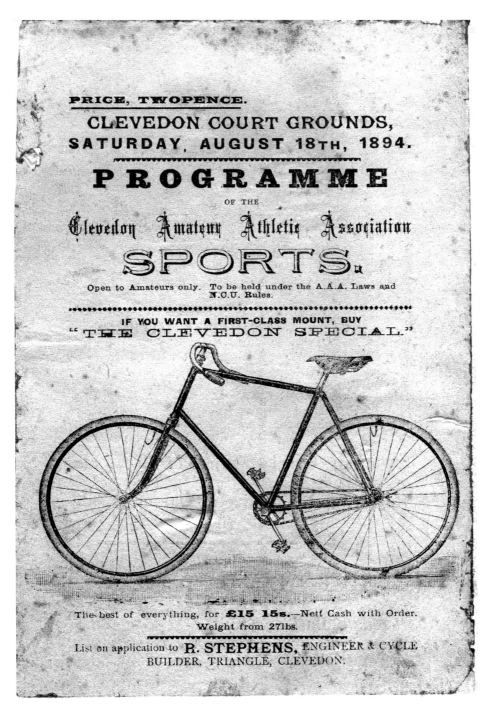

Plate 2.7   The 'Clevedon Special' Bicycle

43

his business, for those five years were to prove the most productive of his career. It does appear that all innovative entrepreneurs have to suffer at least one bankruptcy in their career before achieving success!

Lippincott settled his differences with the Edison-Bell Company, and both parties issued a statement starting:

"-----After several months of friendly negotiation-----"!

Richard also seems to have been relieved of liability for only a month after being declared bankrupt he was working yet again with Edison's British agent.

Chapter 3
Cine and Suspension

Richard Stephens followed developments in the USA with great interest and was still hoping that Edison's ore refining process would gain favour again. From William Dickson he learnt of Edison's progress with the development of a machine to show moving pictures. Dickson had been put in charge of the project and had taken it through several prototype stages.

In 1888 Edison had filed a preliminary patent for a moving picture machine based on a rotating cylinder with multiple pictures printed on it. By 1889 he had a prototype machine working but the length of the performance was limited by the cylinder diameter.

Meanwhile back in England the Bristolian William Friese-Greene had developed and patented a crude cine camera which could also be used as a projector. This camera was unique in that it could take up to ten pictures per second on a strip of celluloid film which was perforated so that it could be quickly moved from frame to frame. The patent was issued on 21st June 1889 as a UK patent and Friese-Greene made the mistake of sending an article about it to Edison. Friese-Greene made several versions of his camera but it was not reliable and because of the low frame rate it was unsatisfactory and so never achieved commercial success.

Because Friese-Greene did not think it worthwhile to patent the concept overseas, Edison was able to exploit the technique in America. By using his vast resources he was able to turn it into a viable technology. He set to work developing a version of his own machine based on a forty-seven foot long strip of celluloid film, about thirty-five millimetres wide. The strip had perforations down each side for transporting the film and this was the basis of the 35mm film used worldwide today for still and moving film production.

Friese-Greene took out a large number of patents relating to cinematography. He patented a system of colour film based on alternate frames being coloured red and green and successfully fought off infringements. This required an appeal to the House of Lords but by the time he had won, his invention had been overtaken by a much improved colour film system. He also patented stereoscopic systems but never succeeded in getting his ideas widely adopted and he died a pauper.

Plate 3.1   *The Edison Kinetoscope*

Although the first model of Edison's modified machine was completed later in 1889 he was still not satisfied with it. When he left America to attend the World Fair in Paris in 1889 he left the project in the very capable hands of William Dickson. By the time he returned Dickson had a working machine ready, and a modified machine was perfected in 1891. It was called the Kinetoscope. (Plate 3.1).

The machine was housed in a pillar-like cabinet with a small slit or window in the top through which the viewer peered. The machine showed a number of scenes each said to consist of about two thousand photographs displayed at forty-six frames per second. The Kinetoscope could not, however, be a commercial success unless suitable films could be made for it.

*Plate 3.2   Number 2, Park Street   Circa 1900
on the right with Sun Canopies*

Dickson therefore had his team develop a camera, and set up a film production company. He also had his own ideas about how films should be shown, believing that the Kinetoscope with its tiny window would not catch on. Dickson was soon suffering from nervous exhaustion and he and Edison fell out. Dickson returned to his native England in 1897 and set up his own film-making companies. In later years he became a renowned film director.

The first public demonstrations of the Kinetoscope were given in America when Edison set up parlours on Broadway in April 1894.

He appointed a European representative, F Z Maguire, who brought Kinetoscopes to Europe. When his ship arrived in the port of Dublin in September 1894 the first European public showing of an Edison moving picture took place. The reporter of the Dublin *Fremman's Journal* compared it favourably with the performance of the actors Irving and Beerbolm Tree and also commented on the amusing effects of the machine when operating in reverse!

Maguire's ship docked in Southampton a week later and he went to the Little Menlo Edison offices in Upper Norwood. In October the first demonstration in London was given in Oxford Street, to much public acclaim. Maguire had several machines with him and sold at least one to Richard Stephens before moving on to give further demonstrations in Paris and other European capitals.

Richard took his Kinetoscope first of all to Cardiff, where demonstrations were given from the middle of December 1894 to the middle of January 1895. He then looked for a suitable location to demonstrate tthe machine in Bristol and eventually hired space from an optician in Park Street. (Plate 3.2).

Alfred H Tooze was a very progressive optician and when he took over the premises of 2, Park Street Bristol in 1894 he invested in the very latest eye test equipment. When he advertised in the local newspaper, the *Bristol Mercury,* offering free eye tests, it came to Richard Stephens' attention. It is not surprising then, that when approached by Stephens to demonstrate the Kinetoscope, Tooze readily agreed.

Number Two, Park Street at that time was a four-storey corner building opposite the newly-opened Council Offices on College Green. In 1976 the building was occupied by the Sue Sheppard employment agency, when a huge gas explosion demolished the adjacent Numbers Four and Six. (Plate 3.3). Number Two was declared unsafe and demolished a few days later, on New Year's Eve.

The site lay derelict for several years until a public protest resulted in Numbers Two and Four being re-built in a facsimile style. (Plate 3.4). At the present time it is still occupied by the Susan Sheppard agency and the same staff members are still employed. It has long been the unrecognised location of the first 'Moving Picture House' in Bristol.

The end of the building where Number Six once stood now has a block-like excrescence attached, which is The Brook Young People's Sexual Health Clinic, whose one redeeming feature is an excellent graffiti by the renowned Bristol artist Banksy. (Plate 3.4, Colour Plate C4).

48

Plate 3.8   The Stephens Family circa 1896

speed' engine for the motor car. They fell out with their backers and so in 1892 they set up their own experimental workshop. It was during this period that Maybach developed the float-chamber carburettor as we now know it, as a means of atomising the fuel which allowed much higher engine speeds to be attained.

To manufacture the car as well as continue with his cycle business Richard needed larger premises so in about 1896 the family moved to

No. 12, The Triangle and established the *Stephens Engineering and Motor Car Works*. Colour Plate C7 shows a hand-coloured postcard from about this time. Here he set up a workshop and started making the components from his design drawings.

Richard, Mary and the children were a close family and quite devout. As well as running the tearooms Mary ran a Bible Class for the Clevedon Baptist Church. A photograph from about this time shows a handsome family grouping, with Percy in a sailor suit and Arthur Ewart wearing a white ruff. (Plate 3.8).

According to the *Clevedon Mercury,* when Clevedon School broke up for the Christmas holidays in 1896 eleven year-old Richard John Stephens, known as R J or Dick, received prizes for drawing and mapping, whilst his friend Archer Ormonde Binding, younger by a year, won prizes for drawing and writing. These skills were to serve them both well for their future careers.

The prototype automobile design had several unique features including an advanced system of independently-sprung front suspension. The engine was rear-mounted and was also completely designed by Stephens. The resemblance to R E Olds' gasoline engines of 1897 is remarkable and it is hard to believe that they did not both stem from their surmised mutual conversations in 1889.

A dog-cart body seating was used in a back-to-back arrangement with the driver and front passenger facing forward and the passengers behind facing backwards. This was a practical solution for vehicles using a rear mounted engine, the arrangement stemming from the rear box area used on carriages for dogs in transit in the horse-drawn era. It had been used by other pioneer motor car manufacturers previously. (Plate 3.9).

In front of the driver was the storage compartment for batteries, tools and waterproof clothing, covered by a bench seat suitable for a child. The engine was a horizontal parallel twin-cylinder of 2,000cc capacity arranged transversely across the back of the car. Drive was by pulley and belts giving two forward speeds. Reverse gear was 'passenger-assisted manual', that is to say, hand-pushed! The engine was high-revving, peaking at 800rpm, giving a bottom gear speed of about 12mph, and a potential top speed of nearly 40 mph. An average speed of 30 mph (on good roads) was typical which was very fast for an early nineteenth century motor car.

Steering was by a bar or tiller arrangement connected directly to the front wheels. The car was fitted with a very advanced independent front suspension running on sliding forks with internal springs which Stephens patented. A large transverse leaf-spring, centre-clamped, was

Plate 3.9   Profile of the prototype Stephens Car

used to link the two front forks, giving additional resilience. This arrangement gave a very comfortable ride, even over Clevedon's rough road surfaces, where the manholes protruded several inches into the air. (Plate 3.10). The car was one of the first to be fitted with independent front suspension, and the first all-British car to be so equipped. The rear wheels were of slightly larger diameter and used semi-elliptical suspension for the solid axle. Owing to the positioning of the crankshaft in relation to the off-side rear wheel, the starting handle had to pass through the spokes.

Wire-spoked wheels were fitted to the prototype, supplied by John Starley who had earlier supplied Richard with bicycles. Brakes could be applied either by foot or manually and could stop the vehicle in its own length. The prototype car was painted in a dark chocolate colour with gold and cream trim lines and the external metalwork was lightly polished brass. These were the colours of the Great Western Railway, as Richard had aspirations to offer his cars to the GWR for hackney carriage work. The seats were furnished with plush red cushions. The car's unladen weight was six and a half hundredweight.(330kg). (Colour Plate C8).

The prototype car was produced in great secrecy and all the early trial runs were carried out at night. It was pushed under covers along Kenn Road, probably to the heath area near the village of Kenn where the trials were carried out on the unmetalled roads. Richard was aware that

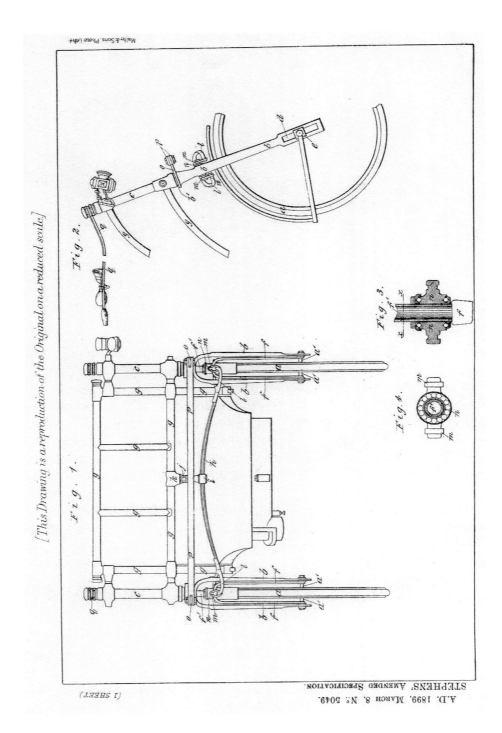

[This Drawing is a reproduction of the Original on a reduced scale.]

Fig. 2.

Fig. 3.

Fig. 4.

Fig. 1.

STEPHENS' AMENDED SPECIFICATION.

A.D. 1899, MARCH 8, Nº 5049.

(1 SHEET)

Plate 3.10   *Extract from Stephens' Patent of 1899*

58

motor car development was advancing rapidly and very competitive. He did not want details of his design to leak until his patent applications were ready. Initially ignition was by hot tubes located under the passenger seat. On one of these nocturnal runs there was some excitement when the seat caught fire and the flames had to be extinguished by rubbing the upholstery on the damp grass verge! This system was later abandoned in favour of electrical ignition but this was at first unreliable and required much testing at night to perfect.

The car was first revealed to the public in 1898 and caused an immediate sensation locally. Mr Edmund Shopland, who had taken over as steam roller driver from Stephens, wrote in his memoir, *Manifold Memories* in 1952:

There was an interesting occasion, in the year 1897, *(sic; probably 1898)* when having an appointment at the Portishead Methodist Church, I found my bicycle tyre punctured. I went down to see what help a friend of mine, Mr R Stephens, who kept a bicycle shop in the Triangle could give me. He could not let me have a cycle, but he offered to run me over in one of his own cars which he had designed and made himself. These cars (with which he eventually ran a service, for a time, between Clevedon and Portishead) had tyres of solid rubber, and were steered by tiller (or handle). I timed the journey of five miles and it took exactly fifteen minutes; this was not a bad performance in those early days of motoring, and before the roads were either water-bound or tar sprayed.

Dick Stephens recalled many years later just how the car worked:

The two-cylinder horizontal engine is of 3.56" (90mm) bore and 6" (152mm) stroke and built into the car frame at the back. A special feature of the engine is the method of controlling the speed. The inlet valves are connected together by links to a bar. In the centre of the bar is attached a strong spring, the opposite end of this spring being attached to a lever. This lever is pivoted and has a cam working on its other end operated by a control lever. Perfect control of the engine is thus obtained by limiting the amount by which the inlet valves can be sucked open. The mechanism has an arrangement whereby one or two cylinders can be used, thus giving another means of regulating power output, which has a maximum value of ten horsepower. (Plate 3.11).

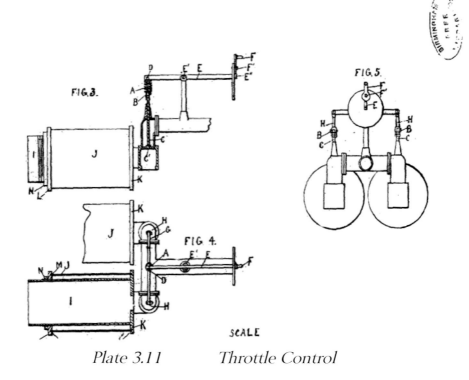

Plate 3.11   *Throttle Control*

The car was not fitted with a carburettor as is now known, but a 'vaporiser', which was a shallow open pan into which petrol is dripped, and over which inlet air was sucked. The vaporiser was situated under the floor behind the front radiator, close to the petrol tank which was on the nearside and round in shape, holding a little over two gallons. The vaporiser was also round in shape, vertical, and on the opposite end, extending below the tank. Petrol was fed from the bottom of the tank to the vaporiser through a short pipe containing a tap. Before the tank was filled this tap was closed, the tank cap screwed airtight and the tap opened. Petrol then fed into the vaporiser until it reached the cover of the petrol inlet pipe, which shut off further supply, feeding more only as used, on the 'bird feeder' principle.

Inside the vaporiser was a float almost equal to the internal diameter. In the centre of this float was a well. The bottom of the float has holes which allow petrol in to the level to which the float is immersed. A tube was fitted to the centre of the float extending upwards and working in a guide tube fixed at the top

60

and extending out to the atmosphere. The engine sucked through a pipe connected at the top into the body of the vaporiser. This caused the air to be drawn down through the centre tube, which then passed out through the small holes in the wall of the tube at the bottom into the well, bubbling through the constant level of petrol in the well, thus creating the necessary vaporisation and producing the gas upon which the engine ran.

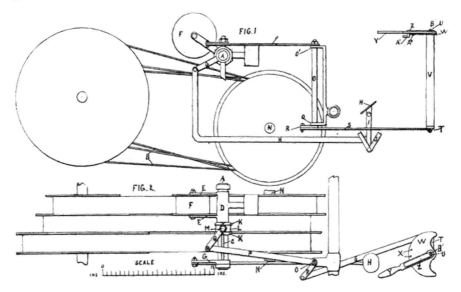

Plate 3.12   Belt Change Mechanism

To assist vaporisation in very cold weather or if the petrol was a little heavy, a pipe was fitted around the inside of the vaporiser at the bottom, one end being connected via an intervening tap to the exhaust box which was immediately behind it. This design of vaporiser required a very close control of petrol density of 0.68 gm/cc, and the driver had to use a densitometer to check the petrol before filling the tank.

The transmission was a drive from the engine shaft via twin belts (Colour Plate C9) giving high and low speeds. The method of engaging the belts was unique and patented, executed by foot pedals. Depression gave the low speed and further depression the high speed. Releasing the pedal resulted in springs pulling the jockey-pulleys to their original positions.' (Plate 3.12).

The brake pedal applied brakes on drums attached to the rear wheels by means of heavy cables attached to small blocks made of hardwood. The brake blocks were mounted in a mechanism which automatically equalised the load on each shoe on all of the wheels fitted with brakes. (Plate 3.13).

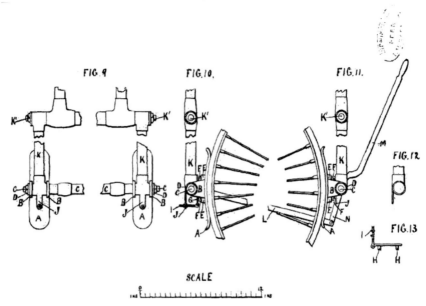

Plate 3.13   Motor Car Brake Equaliser Mechanism

Richard appears to have had a number of teething troubles with the engine and become frustrated with the work required to dismantle it each time. He therefore devised a means of quickly removing the water-jackets from the cylinder heads and he patented this technique. The engine block was fitted with eleven automatic oilers to ensure generous lubrication and a brass oil reservoir was situated just above the engine giving gravity lubrication, as can be seen in Colour Plate C9.

One day in the spring of 1898 as Richard Stephens was working in the yard of his workshop he was startled to hear the putt-putt of an internal combustion engine outside in the road. It drew nearer and entered the yard. It was a bicycle fitted with a single-cylinder petrol engine. It was being ridden by a young man, and running alongside it was Richard's brother Davey. The engine was switched off and the young man dismounted. The visitor was a friend of Davey's from Barry, Charlie Redrup and they had crossed from Barry via the Briton Ferry to Clevedon Pier.

Charles Benjamin Redrup had an unusual history. The son of Harry Redrup a hairdresser and wigmaker, he had been born in Newport South Wales but the family moved to Barry when he was very young. His father had property and was able to give his children a good education. When Charles showed an interest in engineering by building a model steam engine his father considered it might be a good profession to follow. When the boiler exploded and Charles lost the sight of one eye, Harry decided that he needed proper engineering training.

Harry knew that Charles had the aptitude and ability to go on to higher education and this resulted in extensive family discussion. Eventually Charles prevailed and his father, who cut the hair and made wigs for some of the most influential citizens in Barry, was able to arrange for him to be apprenticed to the Great Western Railway for five years as a Premium Engineering Apprentice. There Charles received a first class engineering education and with his natural aptitude to all things mechanical he learnt all aspects of design, drawing, metallurgy, machining, pattern-making, casting and production methods. As well as spending time in the engineering workshops he travelled the network routes as a maintenance assistant. He also acquired a considerable knowledge of electrical engineering which was to stand him in good stead in his future career.

Whilst Charles was still an apprentice Harry bought him a house to use as a workshop. The house was just around the corner from home and Charles built for himself the workshop, the significant features of which were a lathe and other simple machine tools. In this workshop he made a variety of engines in his spare time. It is remarkable that he was to use his home workshops throughout his life to make very intricate engines, and that he did this with the use of only one eye, and, as he once stated, 'with little more than a knife and fork'.

The railway apprenticeship served him well, for when it was completed in the spring of 1897 he signed-on to serve as an Assistant to the Chief Engineer of a cargo ship on a voyage from Cardiff to Philadelphia. His account records that the ship battled force nine gales and hurricanes during the two week journey, and despite being extremely seasick, he attended to the engines and equipment without fail.

Relieved to arrive in Philadelphia, Charles was disconcerted to find that the turn-round was very rapid, and before he had time to recover from his sickness the ship set sail for the return voyage. Fortunately the conditions were less onerous, but on his return to Cardiff, Charles decided that the sea was not for him and he resolved never to take to the water again.

Back in his own workshop Charles Redrup started work on some concepts he had formed during his apprenticeship and later on. His work with steam engines had given him a good insight into motive power but he was anxious to develop an internal combustion engine. He particularly wanted an engine to fit to his bicycle to enable him to get around more quickly. He had heard of the invention in America of the rotary engine, in which the engine block rotates around the crankshaft instead of vice-versa, and was particularly inspired by the work of Fay Oliver Farwell who had built a three-cylinder rotary engine. Farwell went on to design five-cylinder and seven-cylinder rotary engines which were later used by the US military establishments.

Charles realised there was an inherent advantage with this arrangement in that the engine block acted as the flywheel and so the engine could be lighter than a stationary engine. This would be particularly advantageous for a motorcycle where weight is critical. However he wanted to experiment first with a single-cylinder stationary engine so that development problems could be resolved more easily.

He built the engine and successfully bench-tested it. To do so he had to design and build a carburettor and an ignition system from scratch, because the systems used for the early cars were too complicated and bulky for a motorcycle. During his subsequent career he was to be the inventor of a number of novel ignition systems and especially carburettors, which were his particular interest. Finally he installed the engine on the frame of his bicycle and connected it via a belt to a large pulley attached to the rear wheel.

Whilst in Barry, Redrup had made a number of friends with engineering interests including the mining engineer David Stephens, living in Briton Ferry just outside Barry. David had told him about his brother Richard and about his motor car project and had offered to take Charles across to meet him. Charles had jumped at the chance and that is why he had taken his motorcycle to show to Stephens.

Plate C1   ***Richard and Mary Stephens' Wedding,***
Paddington, Australia

Plate C2   *St. Charles Mine Ontario*

South Front of Clevedon Court.

Plate C3   *Clevedon Court Somerset*

Plate C4   Banksy Graffiti on Park Street, Bristol

Plate C5   Elton Crackle-glaze Vase

Plate C6   Elton Tiles around the Clevedon Triangle Clock Tower

Plate C11   ***Sid and Audrey Marks' Collection of Dress Clips***

Plate C12   Charles Redrup age about Twenty-two

***Plate C13   Charles Redrup and Jessie Stacey Driving Tourists
in Burrington Combe***

Plate C14   Richard, Dick and Percy with the John Hunt
Hackney Carriage

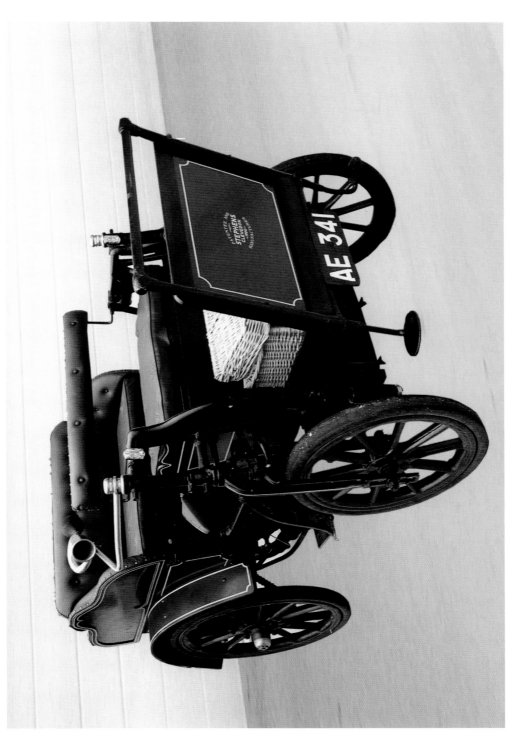

Plate C15   1900 Hackney Carriage Restored by Robin Loder

Plate C16   Clevedon Rifle Club Excursion to Dursley, 1906

Plate C17   *The Patent Automatic Remote Gas Lighter*

Plate C18   Quadruple –Head Automatic Gas   Lighter

Plate C19   Mechanism of Automatic Gas Lighter

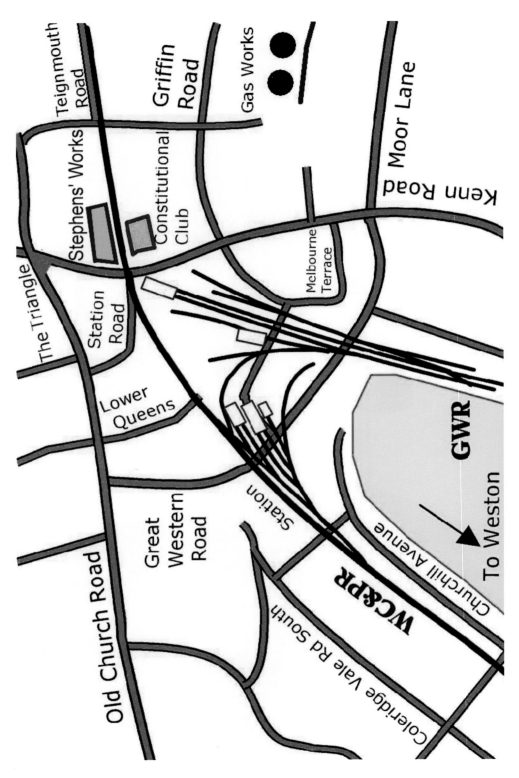

Plate C20   Clevedon Railways in the Town Centre, c1910

MOTOR CARS FOR HIRE.

TELEPHONE 18.y.

R. Stephens, Sons, & Co.,

MOTOR & GENERAL
ENGINEERS, . . .

Patentees and Manufacturers,

Opposite the *G.W.R.*
Station,
CLEVEDON.

**CARS sent to any address at shortest notice
with expert Chauffeur.**

For Terms P.T.O.

Plate C21   1908 Brochure for Model T Taxi Cabs

THE STEPHENS :: IDEAL :: ENGINE STAND

Patented and Registered.

AS SUPPLIED TO

The War Office

AND THE

Royal Aircraft Factory.

No Motor Works or Garage should be without one; it will save its first cost in a very short time.

Clevedon Printing Co., Ld.

One consignment of the Stephens Engine Stand, Model 2, supplied to the order of the Bristol Tramway and Carriage Co., Ltd., Bristol.

The Editor of "The Commercial Motor" writes:—

"We recently had an opportunity to inspect a new engine stand intended for use in the garage and repair shop, which Messrs. Stephen's Engine Stand Co., Clevedon, Somerset, is manufacturing. This stand possesses several very useful features, and is undoubtedly a valuable adjunct to the ordinary plant. With its help, it is possible for one man to dismantle or assemble a heavy four or six cylinder engine. When fixed by the holding-down bolts, the engine can easily be turned over, and, in addition, it can be held and locked in any position required from the vertical.

Short metalling arms connected to the main side frame support the engine. These are, of course, useful in the case of a power unit which is materially heavier on one side than the other, it being easy so to balance the engine that despite any side heaviness it assumes an upright position when in the stand. The locking of the appliance is accomplished by a length of round steel, which fits into a socket cast on one of the main supports, and having at the other end a screwed thread on which two locking nuts can be moved up and down. When tightened up, these nuts hold the frame containing the engine secure from all danger of slipping.

A further feature of interest lies in the bearings which support the main frame. These are not fitted with a top cover, and in consequence when an engine is bolted in position it is possible for it to be lifted completely out of the frame and carried away to the testing bench or wherever it may be required. The whole stand is mounted on four strong rollers.

We were impressed with the solid and simple construction of this new workshop appliance, and have no hesitation in recommending it to garage and workshop owners. There can be little doubt that much time is continually wasted by the assembling and dismantling of engines on the old-fashioned trestles, work which in the ordinary way calls for one skilled man and a couple of labourers.

THE STEPHENS ENGINE STAND CO.,

CLEVEDON, SOMERSET.

Telephone Clevedon 80.   Telegrams: "Stephens, Motors, Clevedon

Plate C22   Engine Frame Brochure 1912

Plate C23   Ewart Stephens in the Royal Naval Air Service
1914 – 1917

Plate C24   Richard and Mary Stephens   c1920

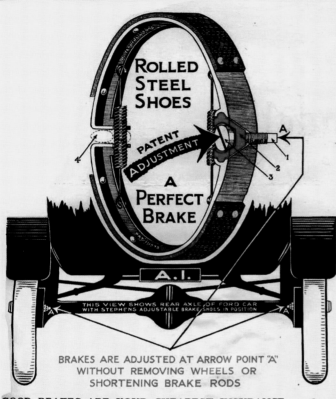
Plate C25   Poster for Stephens Adjustable Brake Shoes 1922

Plate C26   Gold Medal From the 1927 'Emancipation' Run

STEPHENS ADJUSTABLE
BRAKE SHOE

R.STEPHENS & SONS
Pioneers in the Motor Industry

STEPHENS ADJUSTABLE
ENGINE STAND

ADJUSTMENT PERFECTLY SIMPLE
SIMPLY PERFECT

Patentees and Automobile Speciality Manufacturers

AS SUPPLIED TO WAR OFFICE
ROYAL AIRCRAFT FACTORY &C.

115 63 CHURCH ROAD. UPPER NORWOOD. LONDON. S.E.19

AND
CHICAGO.

17th Jan 1929

Lt.Commander M.Grahame White
5A,Montague Mansions
York Street
W.1.

Dear Sir,   Nineteenth Century Motorists

      My son Mr R.J.Stephens tells me he has made
application for membership of the Nineteenth Century Motorists
Circle,but that his application was not accepted.

      I understand from him the qualification for member-
ship is to have driven before the 1000 miles trial of 1900.
If his application was not accepted owing to any doubt that he
had not driven before that date owing to his youth,I should
like to remove any doubt in the minds of the committee in this
respect.

      I therefore beg to state as a definite fact that my
son drove the first car I made when 13½ years of age,and had
done a good deal of driving by April 1900 when he was granted
a license (hackney carriage) to drive a motor car carrying
passengers by the Urban District Council at Clevedon,Som.

      The original license I understand is in his possession
and that he was granted a license should be sufficient evidence
that he had driven considerably before that date.

      There is no doubt my son was the youngest driver of
the period and I have frequently wanted him in years past to
establish the fact through the motoring press.

              Yours faithfully

              R Stephens

Plate C27   **Richard Stephens' Letter to the Circle of Nineteenth
Century Motorists**

*Plate C28   Robert Donat and Margaret Johnston
in AE 174,   in the film 'The Magic Box'*

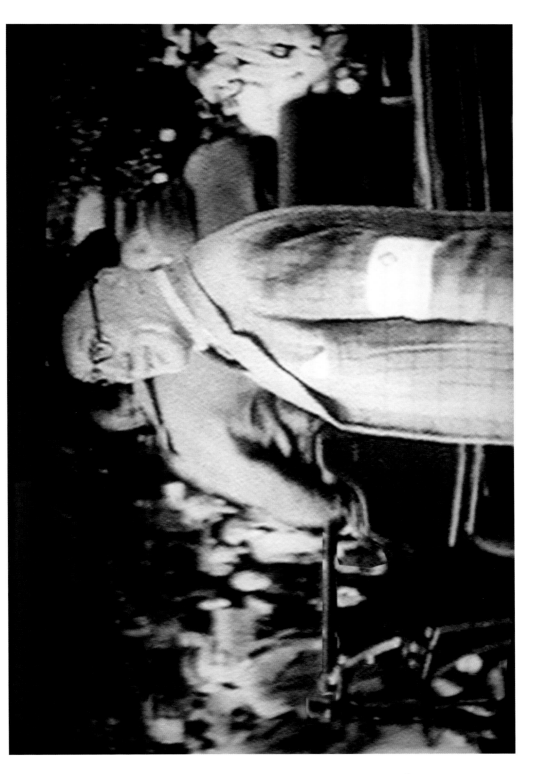

Plate C29   AE 174 in the film 'Genevieve'

Plate C30   Stephens and Son Works in Upper Norwood

Plate C31 Robin Loder and Georgina Westlake Arrive Second
In the 1996 London to Brighton Run

Plate C32   Julia Elton in red hat with AE 174, in Front of the old Stephens Works , now the St Peter's Hospice Shop

Chapter 4
Patents and Praise

Richard was very impressed by Charles Redrup and his work and offered him a job. The prototype car was still under development and was being repaired following a small fire from the hot tube ignition. Hot tube ignition used a device that fitted onto the head of the cylinder to ignite the compressed mixture by means of a flame applied to a tube which protruded into the combustion chamber. The centre of the tube was kept red hot by a burning jet of fuel. The ignitor was a porcelain or platinum tube attached to a plug that fitted into the cylinder head.

The ignitor depended on the fact that on early engines scavenging was poor so that at the end of the combustion stroke the exhaust stroke did not expel all the waste gases. Thus on the compression stroke the piston pushed some left over combustion products into the ignitor tube, followed by fresh fuel-air mixture. When the compression was such that the fuel pushed the waste gases beyond the red hot area of the tube, ignition occurred.

On some designs the ignition timing was adjusted by varying the position of the red hot spot on the tube by moving the burner along the length of the tube. Later designs used a fixed burner and varied the ignitor tube length to alter the timing. Such ignitors had many problems, some caused by the cyclic pressure changes in the tube and the high temperature of the tube leading to fatigue fracture. It was very hard to find materials that were both durable enough for these conditions and inexpensive. Platinum was expensive and to keep costs down, tubes tended to be thin-walled. If the burner flame was too hot it could make the tube white hot, which rapidly damaged the tube and could cause it to burst explosively. This was an easy mistake to make and happened all too often. The open flame of the ignitor heater was also a hazard and probably accounted for Richard Stephens' problems with 'warm' seats! Furthermore the open flame led to a fuel smell around the engine which was not conducive to passenger comfort.

It was not long before Charles Redrup was helping Richard develop an electrical ignition system. Charles was an ingenious inventor and made ignition distributors using epicyclic gearboxes to obtain the correct timing. This was not necessary for a two-cylinder engine, but quite complicated for some of his three and five-cylinder radial engines. For the 1898 Stephens car a contact-breaker and trembler coil were used. Richard installed one of the units in his shop window and connected it to a brass rail mounted vertically next to the door. Children would get a mild shock when they touched it!

During the development of the motor car Richard also dabbled in other things. A patent application for an *Alarm Clock*, No. 12,826 in June 1894 was not proceeded with, but he also helped Sir Edmund Elton to develop a number of items for bicycles. The first of these were for a *Cycle Brake* and a *Rim Brake,* Nos. 23,230 and 27,604 respectively. Until this time bicycle brakes had consisted of blocks of wood pressing on the outside of the tyre, which were made of solid rubber. The invention by John Dunlop in 1888 of the pneumatic tyre made of canvas bonded with liquid rubber took some time to catch on, but by 1896 Dunlop was making cycles using the tyres.

In 1844 Charles Goodyear invented vulcanization by stirring sulphur into a vat of molten rubber. The sulphur produced strong cross-bonds that changed the rubber from the soft natural resin to a strong semi-solid resilient material that was later used for tyres. Just a year later Robert Thomson, a Scottish engineer patented what he called 'aerial wheels'. Thomson's first design used a number of thin inflated tubes inside a leather cover. (Plate 4.1). This design actually had its advantages over later designs. It would take more than one puncture to deflate the whole tyre and varying the pressures could alter the ride conditions. There were no bicycles then, so it would not have been a bicycle tyre that he invented. There were no internal combustion engines either, just a few steam carriages and horse-drawn carriages and carts.

Thomson did some elegant experiments. He fitted his tyres to a carriage and, in Regent's Park in London, had it pulled side by side with an ordinary carriage. He showed it was much easier to pull than the solid-tyred carriage. Expectant observers thought it would be slower because the tyres were soft. However, it was easier to pull and also silent, as it did not make the noise of a solid-tyred carriage. The pneumatic tyres were a technical success but there was no market at the time because rubber was very expensive in the 1840s.

In 1888 John Boyd Dunlop, also a Scott but a veterinarian was watching his young son riding his tricycle on solid rubber tyres over cobbled ground. He noticed that his little boy was not going very fast and did not seem very comfortable. In trying to provide his son with a smoother ride and better handling, Dunlop took the tricycle, wrapped its wheels in thin rubber sheets, glued them together and inflated them with a football pump. That way he laid the foundation for the first

66

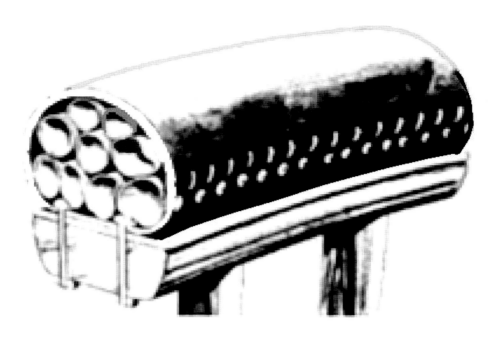

Plate 4.1   *Robert Thomson's 1844 Pneumatic Tyre*

practical and economic pneumatic tyre. Less than a year later Dunlop's invention made its racing debut on two wheels. By enabling a little known rider to easily beat his stronger rivals in a series of bicycle races thanks to the advantage given by his pneumatic tyres, they immediately established the role of motor sports as a feature of the Dunlop heritage.

Dunlop, (Plate 4.2), immediately patented his idea and started to develop his invention into a commercial venture, founding what quickly became known as the Dunlop Pneumatic Tyre Co. Ltd. In 1890 Dunlop opened its first tyre plant in Dublin, Ireland. By 1895 Dunlop tyres were also being sold in Germany, France and Canada, and manufactured in Australia and the USA. By 1898 the business had outgrown its Dublin base, and production was transferred first to Coventry, England and then in 1902 to the 400 acre site in Birmingham, England - later known to the world as Fort Dunlop.

Brakes using blocks on the surface of the tyre were no longer practical and it is known that Dunlop applied for a rim-brake patent at about the same time as Richard Stephens and Sir Edmund Elton. Neither appears to have been granted a patent but both went ahead and used them. The beauty of the brake was that, not only did it run on the inner rim of the wheel, but being a calliper, it automatically equalised the braking force. Rim brakes are now of course universal on all bicycles. The rim brake

Plate 4. 2   *John Boyd Dunlop*

was marketed by Richard and Sir Edmund, and it was advertised as the *Elton Combination Detachable Rim Brake.* It was exhibited at the Crystal Palace National Cycle Show in December 1896 mounted on one of Stephens' celebrated *Clevedon Special Ladies Bicycles.* (Colour Plate C10).

Also on display at the exhibition on one of the Clevedon cycles was another of Sir Edmund Elton's inventions, the *Elton Detachable Dress*

Plate 4.3   Window in Stoke Poges Church.

Guard Clip for Ladies' Cycles. The voluminous dresses worn by women at the time were in great danger of becoming entangled in the wheels and chain of the bicycle and so the clip was designed to keep the folds of the dress away from any moving parts. The *Elton Dress Guard Clip* actually played a minor but not insignificant role in the emancipation of women.

The earliest representation of what could be interpreted as a wheeled frame ridden by a human figure is in the Church at Stoke Poges, famed for the Elegy written in the churchyard by Thomas Gray. It shows a cherub playing a trumpet and riding a wooden frame like a child's hobby-horse. (Plate 4.3). However as only one wheel is shown, it is questionable how the vehicle progressed.

The earliest verified use of a two-wheeled man-ridden vehicle is the hobby horse invented in 1817 by Baron von Drais. He made a walking machine that would help him get around the royal gardens faster. It had two wheels of the same size, being mounted in a frame which he straddled. It was made entirely of wood, including the wheels so was suitable only for riding on smooth paved surfaces such as the paths and roadways in the gardens. He propelled the machine by pushing his feet against the ground. The machine became known as the Draisienne or hobby horse. It did not enjoy great popularity because it was not suitable for travel over any distance between towns or villages. (Plate 4.4).

Plate 4.4   Baron von Drais and The Hobby Horse

The next appearance of a two-wheeled riding machine was in 1865, when pedals were applied directly to the front wheel. This machine was known as the 'boneshaker', (Plate 4.5), since it was also made entirely of wood, then later with metal tyres, and the combination of these with the cobblestone roads of the day made for an extremely uncomfortable ride. The machine was difficult to ride as steering was by the front wheel and it was hard to pedal when going around corners. The use of solid rubber tyres eliminated some of the discomfort of the ride, but the real problem

Plate 4.5   The 'Boneshaker'

was that direct pedal drive to the wheels was too low-geared. This was overcome with the *Ordinary Bicycle* design by James Starley, in which a huge front wheel enabled the gearing to be more appropriate, but this brought a train of its own problems. The problem of steering whilst pedalling remained, whilst sudden braking could cause the rider to somersault head first over the handlebars. (Plate 4.6).

The introduction by his nephew John Starley of a chain-driven sprocket drive to the rear wheels enabled the ungainly *Ordinary* design to be phased out. By 1885 practical *Safety* bicycles were being marketed by his company, Rover, in Coventry. (Plate 4.7).

Riding a bicycle was still not very comfortable, despite efforts made to make sprung saddles and complicated suspensions. John Dunlop's re-invention of the pneumatic tyre in 1888 suddenly opened the riding experience up to a wide range of people, young and old alike, and particularly women.

The bicycle was what made the 'Gay Nineties' gay. It was a practical investment for the working man as transportation, and gave him a much greater flexibility for leisure. Women, heretofore consigned to riding the

Plate 4.6   *The 'Ordinary' Bicycle*

Plate 4.7   *The Rover 'Safety Bicycle'*

Plate 4.8   *Daring Bloomers!*

heavy adult size tricycles that were only practical for taking a turn around the park, now could ride a much more versatile machine and still keep their legs covered with long skirts. However the use of sprocket and chain and the attendant oil made long skirts an encumbrance. One solution was the introduction of bloomers, created by Mrs Amelia Bloomer, voluminous trousers that concealed the most shapely of figures. However to the more conservative of the Victorians they were regarded as shocking, for they revealed to the world the startling fact that women actually had legs! They also enabled women to perform the dare-devil riding tricks of their male counterparts. (Plate 4.8).

Another solution was the dress clip, which kept the skirts away from the moving parts. However even these revealed more than some Victorians were happy with. Nevertheless the movement was unstoppable and within a short time more practical women's wear was adopted and women were freed from the stuffy constraints of Victorian attitudes. The bicycle was taken up with great enthusiasm by the Suffragettes who saw it as a defiant way to demonstrate women's independence, and Cycling Leagues were formed in the UK and USA. In 1896 Susan B. Anthony wrote that:

The bicycle has done more for the emancipation of women
Than anything else in the world.

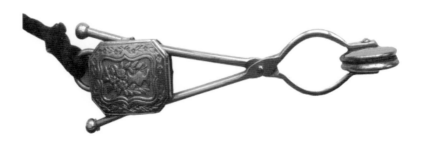

Plate 4.9   *Typical Ladies Dress Clip*

Dress Clips were simple but elegant devices with a decidedly artistic element to them. (Plate 4.9). The Elton-Stephens design was a small clip with fanned vanes which kept the skirts out of the moving chain and cog wheels. No attempt was made to patent the device but its design were so unlike any other Stephens device that it seems certain that Sir Edmund Elton designed them and that Richard manufactured and

74

Plate 4.10   *Appropriate Cycling Attire*

marketed them. The *Clevedon Mercury* reported :

a very ingenious and useful contrivance invented by Mr Stephens.
By its use much trouble and inconvenience are done away with,
the dress guard being capable of removal and replacement in a
moment, thus making easy the work of cleaning and oiling,
which up to date has so tried the patience of lady cyclists.

With the growing emancipation movement women quickly discarded
the long voluminous skirts and bustles for cycling and adopted what was
contemporarily described as 'Appropriate Attire'. (Plate 4.10).

This trend spread also into everyday wear, with long, slim skirts being
considered to meet the desirability of trendiness with modesty. The need
for dress clips for women cyclists soon disappeared and they were
relegated to the history museums and to the collections of a small band
of keen enthusiasts, such as Sid and Audrey Marks of Bristol who have
an excellent collection of dress clips dating from the 1890s and earlier.
(Colour Plate C11).

Early in 1898, shortly after Edmund Shopland's journey to Portishead
in Richard's prototype car, the Stephens family moved across the
Triangle into larger premises, Numbers Nine to Eleven, The Triangle.
Here, in his factory, called *The Clevedon Motor Car and Engineering
Works*, he had room to expand. Mary still retained her Refreshment
Rooms, now at No. 9, whilst Richard set up a production line for his cars
at Nos. 10 and 11.

The Briton Ferry trip was several hours long and so Charles Redrup
commuted from Barry on a weekly basis. Stephens gave Charles
accommodation, together with two other young men whom he had
recruited as apprentices.

The Stephens' household must have been very lively with all of
Richard and Mary's six children still at home, his niece Jessie living
with them and Charles Redrup and two non-family apprentices in
residence.

Whilst Charles Redrup was working for Richard Stephens he was also
encouraged to pursue his own developments. By autumn 1898 he had
completed his design for a rotary motorcycle engine and Stephens
helped him draft a patent application which was submitted in their joint
names. However the application was not granted and Charles started to
devise an alternative approach.

Early in 1899 Stephens applied to have the kerbs outside his
premises dropped to ease the access for his car. He also obtained a

Plate 4.11   Richard Stephens and his Family in the Prototype Car

licence from Clevedon Council to use the car for driving passengers on sightseeing trips. The car was to be seen making trips in and around Clevedon, with Wells, Cheddar Gorge and Burrington Combe being popular destinations. He soon became a familiar sight around Clevedon, driving his family around the town and surrounding countryside. In Plate 4.11 Richard can be seen with Mary in the front seats and Ewart facing them, with Ada and Dick at the back on the rearward facing seats.

However sightseeing was not his prime purpose and now he had a reliable prototype he set about making some production models. He took his two eldest sons Dick and Percy on board as apprentices to join the existing two, Archer Binding and another, name unknown. With these four apprentices and Charles Redrup as general design and manufacturing engineer, he built several models similar to the prototype. Plate 4.12 shows Richard with his team of young apprentices. At the rear on the left is an unknown boy, with Dick and Percy standing next to him. At the front right with the cheeky grin, is Arch Binding, the youngest apprentice, and Dick's former school friend. Arch went on to found his own motor engineering company and lived to be one hundred and five.

Because of his bankruptcy Richard could not raise capital and so Sir Edmund Elton put up the money to enable him to lodge patent applications, purchase materials and pay his staff. Richard's other general engineering activities did bring in some income as did Mary's Refreshment Rooms.

Although he was only thirteen Dick was taught to drive by Richard and soon became expert at handling the vehicle. He was probably the youngest motor car driver of the era. Charles Redrup also learnt to drive the car and would chauffeur paying passengers around the countryside to the popular tourist locations. On these trips he often took Richard's niece Jessie Stacey with him.

In a September 1899 article about the car, *The Autocar* said:

----it has had a severe testing on the roads, with a result considered remarkably favourable by owner and riders alike. The car is something after the style of a dogcart, with seating capacity for three persons, a child and the driver and full loads have been carried some hundreds of miles over an average country without the slightest mishap. The feature of the car of which Mr Stephens is somewhat proud, is the engine, which he has fitted

*Plate 4.12   Richard Stephens and his Apprentices. On the left an
Unknown Boy; Dick and Percy Stephens; Arch Binding on the Right*

himself and which has answered severe tests and now the car is
running daily trips in all parts of the town and neighbourhood.
Petrol is used for fuel with an electric ignition switch which is
simplicity itself in working. The car is steered by a handle and its

passage along the Clevedon streets forms the subject of much favourable comment.

There is a noticeable absence of vibration owing to an ingenious spring arrangement over the front wheels, which, yielding to all road surface inequalities. Manholes, etc – of which there are many in Clevedon, inches above the road level – prevents any jolting worth mentioning being felt by the passengers. The speed is controlled simply by moving a little handle, which is conveniently placed near the driver, an inch one way or another, and the effect on the car can be immediately felt. The chain adjustment is also a good idea, and there are other distinguishing features about the car which make it particularly interesting to automobilists.

Brakes can be applied either by foot or hand, and are strong enough to stop the car within its own length, while the engine can be thrown in or out of gear at will. The spring links, etc, are believed to mark an advance on anything on the road, while nothing could be more simple than the construction of the vaporiser, which we are assured has given no trouble at all since it was fixed. The car has won good opinions from several practical persons, who have tested it, for its quietness in running, handy control, and freedom from some of the causes which at present bother the driver of more than one autocar. Since its completion, the outside fittings of the Stephens car have been plated in places where required, red plush cushions fixed, and the body painted a quiet chocolate colour, with gold and cream lines.

It will be noticed there are no mudguards, except to the front wheels; the water tanks act in this capacity to the hind wheels. There are other points which are deserving of attention, such as the clever arrangement of the tubular members of the framing, and the special means taken to give a sympathetic and easy motion to the front of the car when passing over bad ground. When it is considered how few builders have been able to make a success of their first car, we think it will be admitted that Mr Stephens has earned congratulations over his first automobile.

Shortly after this article was published Richard was approached by a Mr Charles Audrey from Lacock in Wiltshire, who was a wealthy London barrister, to form a company to manufacture cars. The proposal

80

was to inject £6,500 capital by the issue of £1 shares, Stephens to get 3,000 and Audrey and his partners 3,500. Richard would get £1,000 in cash with £2,000 for working capital. Each partner would receive seven and a half percent of net profits. Richard's solicitors, Messrs. Tarr and Arkell, wisely advised against this proposal which would quickly give control of the company to the third parties. It is also unlikely that Richard would have been able to be a director of the company as he was still an undischarged bankrupt.

Chapter 5
Customers and Carriages

Starting and driving the Stephens cars was simplicity itself, although somewhat bemusing at first to a modern driver. Robin Loder who owns the two surviving Stephens cars describes the procedure:

To start the engine first fill up the eleven lubricators with oil. Turn on the petrol tap which supplies fuel to the carburettor, retard the ignition to the correct point, adjust the mixture controls having taken everything into account. Open the throttle lever a small amount. Insert the starting handle between the spokes of the rear wheel and pull the lever up smartly. The engine will not start because the next step is to switch on the ignition. Next pull and it starts at once. After replacing the starting handle, advancing the ignition a little and re-adjusting all the levers it is then the time to climb on board and grasp the tiller with the right hand whilst operating the levers with the left hand.

To move off, by pushing the left pedal forwards the bottom gear belt can be slowly slid over onto the fixed pulley. This takes about three seconds and with the drive taken up and in bottom gear the car is good for about twelve miles per hour. To change into top, keep the throttle open, release the left pedal and the belt slides into neutral. With a nicety of timing the right pedal is depressed and the momentum in the flywheel provides enough power to reach the top gear minimum speed of fifteen miles per hour. In top gear the car will climb most hills and cruise at a steady thirty miles per hour, which on solid tyres and tiller steerage is an adequate speed. At thirty miles per hour the throttle is almost closed and the car runs remarkably quietly.

Fortunately photographs survive of this phase of Richard Stephens' life. Plate 5.1 shows Richard chauffeuring tourists in Clevedon and in Plate 5.2 he is seen standing in front of the car in Burrington Combe. Old Mother Riley appears to be a passenger!

Burrington Combe was a firm favourite tour for visitors. In an earlier epoch it was a cave carved out of the Mendip limestone by an ancient

Plate 5.1   Richard Stephens Drives Tourists Around Clevedon , 1899

Plate 5.2   Tourists at Burrington Combe, 1899

underground river. Thousands of years of erosion had caused the roof to collapse leaving a narrow gorge surrounded by fissured cliffs. It was in one of these fissures that the Reverend Toplady from the nearby village of Blagdon was reputed to have sheltered from a thunderstorm and drawn inspiration for the hymn *Rock of Ages*. The fissure that is believed to have sheltered Toplady is now marked as *The Rock of Ages* and is a popular tourist site.

One of Stephens' regular customers was the Prebendary Vaughan from the Somerset village of Wraxall. Richard would motor over to Wraxall to collect the Prebendary and then take him on long drives. Plate 5.3 shows them setting off on a one-hundred mile run.

Plate 5.3   Richard Sets Off With the Prebendary Vaughan for a 100-Mile Run

The publicity in *The Autocar* brought in a spate of orders, both locally and from as far afield as Oxford. As he manufactured the cars Stephens incorporated modifications, some of a functional nature and some of style. In 1900 he introduced a car with elegantly-shaped sides and more protection for the driver and facing passengers. (Plate 5.4). No record of who purchased this car exists, nor is it seen in any photographs of Richard's own fleet.

Plate 5.4   New Design, 1900

Richard was always keen to advertise his activities and the 7th July issue of the *Clevedon Mercury* contained an item he had submitted:

R Stephens of the Triangle has agreed to show today, Saturday and Monday next, part of the patterns belonging to the motor car and motor, the other parts being still at the foundry for castings, and portions of the car and motor in their complete and also unfinished state.

Later in the year, on September 29th, the *Mercury* contained an item of their own wording:

Motor Cars at Clevedon.

The popularity of Stephens' patent motor cars for the purpose of long or short journeys is beyond question, for they have proved their reliability as a means of progressing whether up hill or down dale, each car doing during the season an average of 50 miles a day. During the past three weeks the largest of the cars has accomplished something like a record for public cars, having travelled no less than 1,026 miles. These figures tell their own tale, and show that the cars are capable of accomplishing everything required of them.

For convenience of country visitors to Clevedon, arrangements have been made for the cars to run evening trips especially on Saturdays to Kenn and Tickenham.

Plate 5.5   Design for Dr Bristow, Wrington

Another elegant design built for Doctor Bristow of Wrington in Somerset had curved rails around the sides. (Plate 5.5). A surviving letter to Doctor Bristow in which Richard gave him a quotation for the car states that the four-seater car would cost £150 whilst the six-seater would cost £180.

A very smart design with the rear-facing seats having cutaway sides was made in 1900 for Mr W N Rowell of Chipping Norton. He was very keen to have the most luxurious fittings and the photograph in Plate 5.6 shows the very plush seat cushions used.

Rowell had an ironmongery business in the High Street of Chipping Norton and an engineering business in Albion Street. He was an astute and wealthy business man and later became Managing Director and

Plate 5.6   *Car for Mr W N Rowell, Chipping Norton* then Vice

Chairman of the Hitchman and Company Brewery in the town. Later in the decade he was to try to become involved in another venture of Richard Stephens and Sir Edmund Elton.

During this busy time at the turn of the century Charles Redrup continued to work for Richard Stephens and as the development work progressed he became more involved with the customers. Whilst the cars were very reliable, they did require servicing and occasional repairs, and Charles became Richard's after-sales service engineer. Initially he travelled to the customers on his motorcycle but this proved inadequate because of the need to carry tools so he used to travel in one of the cars. Perhaps he was the first mobile service engineer!

Charles, who was now a very presentable young man, (Colour Plate C12), was also becoming very attached to Jessie Stacey, Richard Stephens' niece. Colour Plate C13 shows Charles and Jessie chauffeuring tourists along Burrington Combe. The admiring glances of the two onlookers are not to be missed. Perhaps the Stephens car was the first Babemobile!

Charles was also finding that the weekly commute to Clevedon was slowing down his own project, the development of a rotary engine for motorcycles.

His father Harry, whose business brought him in contact with the good and the great around Barry in South Wales, mentioned this to one of his customers, William Graham, (later Sir William), the Assistant Manager of the Tyneside Engine Company which had a works based at the Barry Dock. Graham learnt about Charles' training and experience and in 1902 Charles was appointed as the Company's expert motor engineer in charge of transport and as their electrical engineer. He was thus able to return to Barry and continue working on his project in his own home in his own time.

Charles did not stay long with the Tyneside Engine Company and later in 1902 he went into partnership with a neighbour Alban Richards and set up a company, the Barry Motor Company, to manufacture his rotary engine. By now he was engaged to Jessie who went to live with his parents in Jewel Street Barry, whilst Charles adapted his workshop in Guthrie Street to also provide a home, ready for his forthcoming marriage.

Charles and Jessie were married in July 1903 and Charles went on to have a fascinating career of his own, designing and building engines for motorcycles, cars, boats, buses and aeroplanes. His motorcycle rotary engine, for which he was granted a patent in 1905, was a unique design. It had two cylinders, a pumping chamber and an exhaust chamber

Plate 5.7   *The 'Barry' Engine*

forming a cross arrangement, the pumping chamber acting as a supercharger.

The crankcase was the inlet manifold and the mixture was forced from the pumping chamber into the active cylinder through a valve when the two pistons went to bottom dead centre. The active cylinder then compressed the mixture whilst the spent charge from the other cylinder was forced into the exhaust chamber via another valve. In all, the cycling was effected by a pair of valves on each cylinder. Later versions used a rotary valve. The whole cylinder block rotated about a fixed crankshaft and drove the rear wheel of the motorcycle via a belt. (Plate 5.7).

Two motorcycles were exhibited in the Burners Hall exhibition in 1904 and declared to be a marvel. (Plate 5.8). The brochure offered engines rated at between three and fifty horsepower, prices starting at sixteen guineas. Complete motorcycles were also on offer at from 40 to 52 guineas. An American visitor to the exhibition offered Charles a contract to take the engine to America but his partner Alban Richards demurred.

Plate 5.8   The 'Barry' Motorcycle on Display in Burners Hall

At the same time Charles had developed a small two-cylinder contra-rotating 'Reactionless' aero engine which was demonstrated to the Royal Balloon Factory at Farnborough in 1906. This was followed by two or three larger engines of three, five and eventually one of seven cylinders which was demonstrated to the Royal Flying Corps in 1912.   The interest roused spurred Charles on to design a huge contra-rotating reactionless engine of 150 horsepower. This was tested in 1914 by the Air Board who showed great interest but requested that a stationary radial engine be developed from it. Later in 1914 this radial engine was tested and the Air Board put Charles Redrup in contact with Vickers Aircraft who contracted to develop and manufacture it.

The 'Hart Engine' as it was known, took far longer to develop than imagined, mainly due to Vickers being aircraft manufacturers and having little practical experience of engine development. The engine was eventually installed in a Vickers FB12c aircraft in 1917. (Plate 5.9). However two factors conspired against success. The production jigs, ordered from America, were lost when the transport ship was torpedoed. Furthermore, by this stage of the War pusher aircraft were no longer the vogue and the Air Ministry decided to concentrate production on SE5A and Sopwith Camel aircraft, so the engine never went into production.

*Plate 5.13   Charles Redrup Seated in the Bristol Tramways Bus
Fitted with the Redrup RR4 Engine*

95

Plate 5.14   Bristol Tramways and Carriage Company Axial
Wobble-Plate Engine

Charles Redrup's last engine was a one-thousand horsepower axial cam engine. He made this in his workshop but it appears that it was never actually run. With deterioration of his good eye and the onset of senility he retired quietly with Jessie, visited from time to time by his seven children, and died in 1961 at the age of eighty-three. Several of Charles Redrup's engines still exist and are on display in the Manchester Museum of Science and Industry.

The Author's book *The Knife and Fork Man* tells the full story of Charles Redrup's fascinating career.

Despite his thriving business, Richard Stephens still had time for external interests. As a boy in Cwmbran he had been in the town band. During his time in Canada he had played the trumpet and once settled in Clevedon, he took it up again. Around the turn of the century he became Honorary Secretary of the Clevedon Town Band which practised in the Engineers' Drill Hall on Moor Lane three nights a week. He also joined the local Chamber of Commerce.

At about the same time Richard and Mary's eldest daughter Ada got married to a grocer, Harold Tarrant, whom she had met in Bristol, and they set up home in Weston-super-Mare where she, together with her mother Mary, joined the Boulevard Congregational Church Choir. Ada became an accomplished soprano singer in the town. The second daughter Cecilia married Phillip Day, a butcher from Hampstead and they set up home for a time at Number 10, The Triangle. In 1900 their first son Phillip Ewart was born.

Ethel, the youngest daughter had taken a fancy to a man who was eight years her senior, Ted Winter, a local watchmaker and jeweller who drove occasionally for Richard. In August 1900 one of Stephens' cars had the first accident ever to happen to one of his vehicles. The car was being driven by Ted Winter with Arch Binding's father Thomas as passenger. Thomas Binding had a carrier business in Kenn Road Clevedon and drove a horse and cart service to Bristol every day from outside the Three Kings public house. In later years he ran the service using motor vehicles and was still going strong in 1923.

Ted Winter was driving Thomas quietly along Green Beach, and just passing a house called 'Fairfield', when they overtook another vehicle. This took the car close to the offside kerb. Just at that moment a large black dog ran off the pavement and got under the front wheels of the car. Ted instinctively swerved and the car struck against the kerbing with such force as to throw the occupants out. They suffered little or no injury but the car was caused considerable damage. The covering was removed and the car loaded onto a cart and returned to the workshop.

The front wheel was broken off at the forks and found to be twisted and bent. The second wheel also on the same side was bent and the spokes knocked out. Dick Stephens straightened out the forks and effected a braze repair, the total cost amounting to about ten pounds. History does not record the fate of the dog, but the incident did not endear Ted Winter to Richard who already disapproved of his attentions to Ethel.

Chapter 6
Hackneys and Hills

The prototype Stephens car had become widely known in the area around Clevedon and several people had made purchases. However Richard was about to make a sale which would ultimately result in him starting yet another business.

Close to Clevedon, the City of Bath was also a hilly place, frequented by visitors to the Spa and inhabited by wealthy merchants, landowners and gentry. It was a retirement resort for the elderly and indeed, the bath chair gets its name from the city. Richard Stephens realised that the hilly streets of Clevedon and Bath were well suited to motorised travel and set out to develop these markets.

Sometime during 1899 a Mr Byrom from Bath ordered a car and it went into manufacture during 1900. A friend of Byrom's in Bath, John Hunt, who ran a horse-drawn hackney carriage business, heard of the Stephens cars and visited the works in Clevedon to see Byrom's car being built. He enquired about a larger version of the car for use as a taxi and placed an order. He was invited to work on the Byrom car to familiarise himself with its workings. The four-seater design was therefore followed by a mechanically-similar but slightly larger six-seater.

John Hunt applied to the Watch Committee in Bath for a Hackney Carriage licence and this was strongly opposed by the horse-drawn hackney drivers. However Dick Stephens junior, although only fifteen, gave Hunt driving lessons and in May 1900, on Whit weekend, Dick drove the new vehicle to Bath to demonstrate it to the Watch Committee. As it drove through the city John Hunt was jeered by the hackney carriage drivers. "He'll fall to bits before the week is out!" shouted one cab driver. "It's a seven day wonder!" cried another as the car spluttered past the rank of frightened cab horses. "They'll be telling us next that the horse is finished!" was the derisory call. There was tremendous public opposition to John Hunt as Dick vouched to the Committee for Hunt's ability to drive. However the Committee were not to be put off by this display of opposition and were not intimidated. They were so enthralled that the licence was granted without further ado. It was the first motorised hackney carriage to ply the streets of Bath. (Colour Plate C14).

Stephens had ideas of his own of running a hackney carriage service and so he set about building more six-seater cars for his own use and also some nine-seater buses. He had his hackney stand in front of the clock on the Triangle in Clevedon and was soon busy. (Plate 6.4).

Richard's tourist trips were also very popular and good value for money. For short circular tours around the town he charged two shillings per head per hour for parties of four, whilst short trips to and from the beaches cost sixpence one way. He charged one pound per person for a round trip to Cheddar Gorge, where Gough's Cave was a popular destination, (Plate 6.5), and one pound ten shillings to Wells and back for a four-passenger load. Trips further afield to Taunton or Gloucester cost two pounds ten shillings and three pounds each.

One trip which was recorded about twenty years later in his book called *The Autocar-Biography,* was by Owen John, who wrote the *On the Road* column in the *The Autocar.* His full name was Owen John Llewellyn and he was the son of Colonel Llewellyn from Wrington in Somerset who is reputed to have bought a Stephens car in 1900. Owen John recalled a trip to the Great Bath Horse Show, driven by Richard Stephens. He remarked the car was normal, insofar as it had four wheels, but that the seats were:

disposed like the Cherubim in the Book of Revelations, being two in front facing backwards, two ditto facing forwards, and two behind facing rearwards. It had a linen scalloped canopy on the lines of the sun-awnings that keep the ices cool on ice-cream barrows.

He went on to add that the carburettor was exactly like a coffee-making machine! Only the hackney carriages had the engine cover opening like that of a grand piano so Llewellyn's ride must have been one of these, as is apparent from his next comments:

on the level there was nothing for many miles to beat it and of most inclines it heeded little; it was only when one took it amid the Mendips that it gave trouble, and then it became necessary---- to open the piano-like back and to throw resin, or dust into the spaces between the rollers and the belts. This made the latter "bite", and off the car used to go and leave us all behind. However, the driver, hanging on by the tiller, always managed to get in, and he would invariably be found waiting for us at the top.

Plate 6.5   Richard with Honeymooners at Gough's Cave

On arrival at the Show they were greeted with consternation:

We were the Writing on the Wall - if the rest of the company had only realised it. We were the Future, the Sign of the Times, the Red Flag on the Horizon - and we were warned away from the entrance gate. The police were powerless, but the stewards and all their myrmidons rallied to the rescue of the old order of things. With tears in their eyes, they begged and beseeched us to come no further, and of course, we agreed, and so the New Order of Things was stabled far away, and after all the jumping and the trotting and the cantering and the merry tinkle was over, we had to rejoin Mr Stephens by stealth far from the Show Ground, and so left Bath and its Horse Show in peace once more.

By 1832 railways had spread from the industrial heartlands of Britain, Birmingham and Manchester, northwards to Scotland and southward to London and Gloucester. However there was no link from London to the South West of England, Bristol or further into Somerset, Devon or Cornwall. Thus in that year a group of entrepreneurs started to raise finance and founded the Great Western Railway Company by Act of Parliament in 1835. Design work was already well under way and routes surveyed when in 1833 an engineer was employed to manage the construction. Isambard Kingdom Brunel was the son of a tunnelling engineer, Marc Isambard Brunel, and already had considerable experience of excavation, tunnelling and project management.

However he was not only a civil engineer but also a designer of the highest calibre. By force of personality and good argument he persuaded the Board of the Company to abandon the standard gauge of four feet eight and a half inches (1435mm) and to adopt a wider gauge of seven feet. (2140mm). He argued, perceptively, that as locomotives continued to develop, higher speeds would be attainable on the wider gauge and passengers would be less subjected to swaying and vibration.

The Company had a vision of connecting London to New York by rail and steamer and a gigantic ship was constructed, also by Brunel. *The Great Western* was launched in 1837 and started the trans-Atlantic service in the same year, even before the railway was completed.

Simultaneous construction of the double-track line took place with two sections, from Bristol to Bath and from London to Reading via Maidenhead. The London-Maidenhead section was the first to open in 1838 and the whole line from London to Bristol was finished in 1841.

Plate 6.6   Isambard K Brunel before the first attempt to launch
the 'Great Eastern' at Millwall

Plate 6.7   Stephens and Apprentices with a Canopied Car

Brunel designed huge terminal buildings at Paddington and Temple Meads in Bristol and a locomotive works at Swindon which was opened in 1843. The first locomotive to come out of the works, designed by Daniel Gooch, was also named *Great Western*. Gooch designed all their main rolling stock and after thirty-three years was made Chairman of the GWR.

More ships were added to the fleet with the first all-iron steamship the *Great Britain* starting a revolution in ship design. The sister ship to the *Great Western* was even larger and named the *Great Eastern*. It was intended to travel to the Far East but with this design Brunel may have over-reached himself for it gave continuous trouble. (Plate 6.6) Branches of the broad gauge line spread across the West Country including the link to Clevedon, but the writing was on the wall. The incompatibility of narrow and broad gauges led to delays and high costs. The problem was exemplified by the junction at Gloucester where the Birmingham narrow gauge railway terminated and Brunel's wide gauge met it. Passengers had to transfer from one train to another if they wished to travel from Bristol to the Midlands or the North West.

In 1846 the GWR was prevented from building any more broad gauge. Many hundreds of miles of track had third rails laid so that rolling stock of either gauge could use it, but the broad gauge track was progressively lifted. The last broad gauge track was finally removed in

Plate 6.8   'Charabanc' Hackney and Canopied Car
At Green Beach, Clevedon

1892 and thousands of locomotives and other rolling stock were scrapped.

To access South Wales travellers had to pass through Gloucester until the GWR opened a tunnel under the Severn in 1886 and linked Bristol and Cardiff directly. The GWR had mines near Pontypool to provide a risk-free source of coal and this link enabled the coal to travel more quickly than having to take the loop through Gloucester.

Brunel suffered a stroke on board the *Great Eastern* in 1859, just as she was about to sail on her first voyage to New York. He died in London a few days later. Perhaps the greatest tribute to Brunel is the Clifton Suspension Bridge in Bristol which took over thirty years to build owing to financial constraints and was not opened until five years after his death.

The main line GWR Bristol to Exeter railway via Yatton was opened in 1841 and on the same day a branch line to Weston-super-Mare was opened. A further branch line was built from Yatton the Clevedon in 1847 and in 1867 the Bristol to Portishead Branch line opened but there was no direct link from Weston to Clevedon or Portishead. For several years Stephens ran hackney carriage services from Clevedon to Portishead and Weston-super-Mare stations, until a GWR link from Portishead was built.

Richard's contract price For the return trip to and from Portishead was two shillings per person for a full car. Other prices varied depending on the number of passengers. This was a very lucrative trade until the GWR extension from Portishead opened in 1907. There was great demand for an extension from Portishead which was a very busy town, and to Weston-super-Mare which was a popular holiday resort. Richard therefore also ran a service to and from Weston.

For the summer weather Richard designed canopies to keep the sun off his passengers. These were the ones referred to by Owen John in his book *The Autocar-Biography*. The team of stalwart apprentices made and fitted them to the cars. (Plate 6.7). They were particularly popular for the runs to the beach at Clevedon and to Weston. Some of the later vehicles were fitted with side steering wheels instead of the tiller bar. (Plate 6.8).

Whilst the hackney carriage built for John Hunt of Bath had a rear-facing back seat, his later hackneys had rear-entrance 'tonneau' type rear ends with a mixture of side-facing and forward-facing seats as can be seen from the photographs taken outside Portishead station, Plate 6.9, and on Holly Lane, Plate 6.10.

One problem that had recurred time and time again when Charles Redrup was making his after-sales calls was damage to the wire-spoked wheels. The cars were fitted with solid rubber tyres but this was not a problem generally because of the smooth suspension. When Richard or his regular drivers drove the cars they were very careful to use reasonable roads, travel at speeds appropriate to the road conditions, and to avoid bumps and kerbs. However private owners were not always so careful and the spoked wheels combined with solid tyres became somewhat of a problem. Later cars were fitted with more robust wooden wheels. (Plate 6.10).

In 1903 Richard built two nine-seater omnibuses for the Clevedon to Portishead routes. The bus service was to replace a coach and horses service previously ran by a Mr J Brown. The buses were based on the hackney carriage design, had the wooden wheels, and the driver sat in a 'casket' at the front. He had a steering wheel but it was at the side attached directly to the top of the front offside wheel mounting shaft and drove it directly via a bevel. From the photographs it looks rather awkward to use. In 1905 as winter approached he converted these buses to have enclosed cabins. (Plate 6.11).

Plate 6.9   Stephens Hackney Carriages
At Portishead Station 1902

*Plate 6.10   Cars with Wooden   Wheels and
Steering Wheels at Holly Lane, 1903*

The wooden wheels were made by Richard himself, as the *Clevedon Mercury* reported on 6th February 1904:

A NEW industry of much promise has lately been started at Clevedon, at the motor works of our enterprising townsman, Mr R Stephens, Triangle. It has to do with the manufacture of wheels for motor, carriage and other purposes, they being made of wood with iron ribs (sic) and rubber tyres. They are planned and built on the premises, and several improvements are introduced in their construction.

The reference to iron 'ribs' is clearly a mis-print, and should be 'rims', as can be clearly seen from the Plates.

Richard's two elder sons Dick and Percy were now working with him full time and were accomplished, if sometimes erratic drivers. In a letter to *The Autocar* in the 1950s Dick recalled that in about 1903 he had been driving a car with pneumatic tyres along Victoria Street in Westminster. The solid-tyred cars that he was used to driving had no tendency to skid but on this occasion, after it had been raining, he had to stop suddenly. He locked his brakes and went round in a complete

111

Plate 6.11   Stephens Autobus with sons Dick and Percy

circle to his acute embarrassment and the amusement of the onlookers.

In July 1905 he was caught doing 26mph in a 20mph area near Basingstoke, driving a 24 horsepower, 4.6-litre Léon Bollée car. He was fined three pounds with twelve shillings costs. As business had flourished Richard had bought a 24 horsepower Napier car which he used both privately and for family members to drive for the business, and in February 1906 Dick was fined four pounds with two shillings costs for exceeding the 10mph speed limit in Hyde Park with this car.

A few years later Dick was driving the Napier in the Grampians in mid-winter. One of the rear wheels had an anti-skid device, a steel-studded cover which worked well on muddy roads. However on icy roads and a steep descent when he tried to brake the wheels skidded. Pumping the brakes he managed to get to the bottom of the gradient at ever-increasing speed, and just managed to negotiate the steep bend at the bottom.

In Bath John Hunt up-rated his taxi cabs to use the Ford Model B and in 1903 sold the original hackney back to Richard Stephens who added it to his fleet. Richard took the opportunity to fit it with a conventional carburettor, a French Longuemare which he had been progressively fitting to his other vehicles since 1902. This was because the vaporisers used low-density spirit whose density had to be carefully checked before each trip to ensure it was within limits. Car and bus drivers were now expecting motoring to be simpler and carburettors eliminated the need for these checks. The spirit was also becoming scarcer whilst petrol was more readily available.

By now Richard Stephens had a thriving private car hire business and motor works that were a major feature in the town centre of Clevedon. He was also an upright citizen having expunged his misdemeanour of chalking advertisements on the pier! Around this time he became a Freemason, joining the Coleridge Club and also joined the Constitutional Club, eventually becoming a committee member.

He was now advertising regularly in the *Clevedon Mercury* for his hire car and bus services. One timetable which was circulated alluded to the risk of unreliability in maintaining the schedule:

The Time Table shows the times at which the Cars may be expected to arrive and depart, but their arrival and departure at the times stated is not guaranteed, nor do the proprietors hold themselves responsible for any delay, or any consequence arising therefrom

This Time Table shows the times at which the Cars may be expected to arrive and depart, but their arrival or departure at the times stated is not guaranteed, nor do the Proprietors hold themselves responsible for delay, or any consequence arising therefrom.

CARS FOR PRIVATE PARTIES.

Table of Fares—

Short Circular Tours for Parties, 2/- each per hour.
(Not less than 4).

Beach to Station (or vice versa)	6d. each.
Green Beach to Parish Church (stop or return)	6d. each.
Portishead (return journey , not less than 4 ...	2/- each.
Yatton or Tickenham (return journey), not less than 4	2/- each.
Weston-super-Mare or Bristol (double journey)	15/-.
Cheddar (return journey)	£1 0 0
Wells (return), £1 10s. ; Taunton (return)	2 10 0
Gloucester (return journey)	3 0 0
Hire by Day of 9 Hours ; other Journeys by arrangement.	

MOTOR CARS

IMPROVED SERVICE BETWEEN
CLEVEDON & PORTISHEAD

WILL RUN DAILY (SUNDAYS EXCEPTED).

TIME TABLE FOR JULY & AUGUST, 1906.

G.W.R. STATION.

Clevedon, depart 9.40, 11.15 a.m., 2.0, 3.30, 5.0, 7.45 p.m.

Portishead, arr. 10.10, 11.45 a:m., 2.30, 4.0, 5.30, 8.15 p.m.

Portishead, dep. 10.20 a.m., 12.58, 3.20, 5.0, 6.7, 8.20 p.m.

Clevedon, arr. 10.50 a.m., 1.27, 3.50, 5.30, 6.37, 8.50 p.m.

Return Fares, 1/6 ; Single, 1/-

Plate 6.12 Timetable of Cars and Car Hire

Clearly Product Liability was an issue even in those days! This advertisement also shows a placard for Ted Winter's business. By this time Richard had overcome his misgivings, as in 1902, Ted had married Ethel, and they now lived next door to Richard and his remaining family. Ted shared the workshop and undertook watchmaking and the sale of jewellery and all kinds of related activities such as engraving and plating. (Plate 6.12). The advertisement also had a clause:

The prices for the various journeys are also displayed.

Chapter 7
Licences and Lighters

In 1865 in Britain, the 'Locomotives on Highways Act' was introduced. Better known as the 'Red Flag Act', it was aimed primarily at the heavy steam traction engines which could cause considerable road damage and frighten the horses of other road users. The act stipulated that all mechanically powered road vehicles must have three drivers, one to drive, one to stoke so that the driver could concentrate on the road, and one to walk fifty yards in front, carrying a red flag to warn other road users. The vehicles were restricted to four miles per hour (6.4 kilometers per hour) on the open road and two miles per hour (3.2 kilometers per hour)) in towns.

An Act of 1878 did away with the red flag, but the vehicle still had to be preceded by a man on foot to warn drivers of horse-driven coaches. In 1896 the act was withdrawn and the speed limit increased to fourteen miles per hour. (22 kilometers per hour). To mark the event a stream of cars set off for an 'Emancipation Run' from the Hotel Metropole in London to the Hotel Metropole in Brighton, which was a hazardous undertaking in those days. Plate 7.1 shows the Cannstatt Daimler 'Present Times' car outside the Hotel Metropole, Brighton, on Monday 16th November, two days after the completion of the 'Emancipation Run' on the Saturday. The driver is Johannes van Toll, whilst on the rear seat wearing the hat is Gottlieb Daimler. The other rear-seat passenger is possibly Alfred Ledger, a founder member of the ACGB&I. (Automobile Club of Great Britain and Ireland).

The trip is remembered annually in the Commemoration Run from London's Hyde Park to Brighton. Whilst not a race, drivers do take pride in arriving as early as possible at the sea front, prior to the commemorative dinner!

Heavy vehicles were still subject to lower speed limits and the *Clevedon Mercury* records that in April 1898 Edmund Shopland, who had taken over the steam roller driving from Richard Stephens, was summoned for driving through the neighbouring village of Nailsea at speeds in excess of two miles per hour!

In 1903 a new Motor Car Act required all motorised vehicles used on public roads to display a registration plate with effect from the first of January 1904. This was to facilitate the identification of any vehicle and

116

Plate 7.1 Cannstatt-Daimler Car in the 1896 Emancipation Run

owner involved in a traffic accident, or any civil or criminal misdemeanour. The motor taxation was based on horsepower. The Act was piloted through the House of Commons by the father of the present Lord Montagu of Beaulieu, who negotiated a relaxation in the speed limit as a quid pro quo, to twenty miles per hour.

Richard Stephens' vehicles were allocated registration marks by the Bristol County Borough Council. Major cities or areas of population had registration marks beginning with the letter 'A' and for Bristol the letters 'AE' were allocated. Thus the Stephens first prototype car received the registration AE 174, and the hackney carriage re-purchased from John Hunt in 1903 was given the registration AE 341.

The 1903 Act also laid down other standards such as lighting for driving at night. The driving licence was also introduced and Richard was one of the first motorists to obtain one. The Act however stipulated that the minimum age for a driver was to be seventeen and so Dick, who had been driving since he was thirteen and a half and who turned seventeen in August 1902, only just scraped in by the skin of his teeth! Percy had to wait until 1904 and Ewart until 1908 to get their licences.

The licence had to be applied for in the County or County Borough in which the applicant resided. This was in contrast to the application for the registration plate, which could be made in any part of the country. The driving licence cost five shillings and had to be renewed annually. One of the more valuable concessions that was negotiated, was that a licence could not be endorsed after the first or second speeding offence.

Sir Edmund Elton was one of Richard's regular customers and being a keen cyclist he made use of Richard's services for repairs and maintenance. An invoice for early 1906 survives and reads as follows:

One tin of bicycle oil	6d
Making of two iron washers	1s 0d
New cover 9s 6d and chain 2s 6d	12s 0d
One piece of ¼" cast steel 14" long	3d
Adjusting wheel	4d
Repairing tyre	6d
Total	14s 7d

Another invoice from March to October 1906 totals 12s 10d!

Richard Stephens continued with his motor and cycle repair business and his car hire service for several more years. He still ran special outings and modified his cars as new ideas came to him. A contemporary photograph from 1906 shows a party of the Clevedon Rifle Club setting off for an outing to Dursley in these two vehicles. The new larger headlamps can be clearly seen, as can large battery boxes carried on the running boards. AE 174 also had a steering wheel at this time although AE 341 still had the tiller. (Colour Plate C16).

Fortunately things were about to improve and Richard would soon be sending Sir Edmund some much larger invoices. Whilst he was running his cycle and motor businesses Richard was also working with Sir Edmund on a completely different project.

Sir Edmund, who was Chairman of the Clevedon Gas Company, was concerned at the cost of the gas wasted when the lamps were lit and extinguished at dusk and dawn. Because of the time taken for a lamplighter to complete his rounds, a need which occurred all across the nation, local authorities had to start and stop the lighting process at a legally decreed time, called 'Lighting Up Time'. This was defined as starting half an hour before dusk and half an hour after dawn. In practice, because of the length of the lamplighter's round he often had to set out in the evening in broad daylight to start lighting the lamps. Similarly he could not start to extinguish the lamps until it was almost daylight, and he finished his round when it was very light.

Sir Edmund conceived of an idea whereby the lamps could be extinguished remotely and engaged Richard Stephens to help him develop and patent the idea. They submitted a patent application on the Second of July 1906 and the patent was granted on 23rd May 1907. This was a much more rapid turnaround than present patent applicants receive!

The concept was   brilliantly simple. Each gas lamp was fitted with a pressure-activated valve to turn the gas on and off. In the evenings a pressure pulse to the gas pipeline was injected at the Gas Works and this tripped the valve from the 'off' to the 'on' position. The following morning another pressure pulse was injected and the valves all switched to the 'off' position. These operations could be carried out at the very moment of 'Lighting Up Time', saving significant quantities of gas.

The device worked by having a pilot light next to the main light to ignite it. The valves to the two lights connected to an arm such that when the pilot light was on, the main light was off, and vice-versa. The

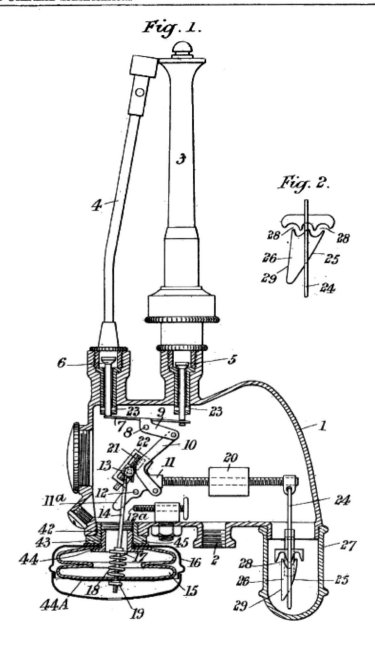

Fig. 1.

Fig. 2.

Plate 7.2   *The Patent Automatic Remote Lamplighter*

end of the arm was connected to a bellows which was subject to mains pressure. When the pressure pulse in the mains entered the bellows it kicked the arm from one position to the other. The speed of the operation was adjusted so that the main light lit before the pilot light extinguished, and on shutting down, the pilot light was lit before the main light went out. (Plate 7.2 and Colour Plate C17).

Although they didn't know it, Sir Edmund and Richard had invented the 'bi-stable' or 'flip-flop', a device that can be switched from one state to another by an input signal and back again by another signal. They are a basic form of 'positive feedback', in which an output is used to re-inforce the input signal. Although positive feedback has uses as in the bi-stable, it is generally undesirable, as anyone who has held a microphone too close to a loudspeaker of a public address system can vouch! Such devices were later made in electrical form and now form the basis of the micro-processor used in digital computers worldwide.

The Patent No. 15,067 for *Improvements in Apparatus to be used in connection with Gas Lamps for Lighting and Extinguishing from a Distance* was for a single lamp, (Colour Plate C17), but it was followed by two more patents. Many road junctions and town centres required multiple lamp heads and so these were also developed. One very popular design had three automatic heads and an additional lamp that was permanently lit. (Colour Plate C18). Colour Plate C19 shows the operating mechanism.

These developments required a good deal of investment and even Sir Edmund was hard pushed to finance the project. Richard and his son Percy developed the prototype 'lighters' as they were called, and costs started to mount. Richard and Sir Edmund agreed to split the development costs. Richard's invoice for work from August to December 1906 came to £54 14s and fourpence-halfpenny, so Richard charged Sir Edmund £27 7s and twopence-farthing! Even farthings counted in those days.

During 1906 a few trial gas lighters were installed in Highdale Road Clevedon. The bill from Richard for January to April 1907 came to £101 19s 10d, and Sir Edmund's share of this was £50 19s 11d. Richard and Percy's time was charged at thirty shillings per fifty-one hour week. The charges included two trips to Bristol at 6s and 10s respectively.

William Rowell, who had purchased a Stephens car in 1900 and who still kept in touch through his servicing needs, got to hear about the project and expressed a willingness to invest. In May 1907 Richard visited Rowell and proposed a Syndicate whereby Rowell would invest five thousand pounds in return for shares in the business. He would also undertake the manufacture of the lighters. Of this sum, Richard and Sir Edmund would receive two thousand pounds each and Percy would receive one thousand pounds.

Sir Edmund's eldest daughter Kathleen was married to a stockbroker Guy Kindersley and he undertook to organise the syndication. However Rowell delayed and prevaricated, and Richard became suspicious of his motives. By September Rowell had put forward a revised proposal for the deal but Guy Kindersley's analysis showed that, although at first glance it looked an attractive deal, on detailed examination it had several pitfalls. In a letter to Sir Edmund Elton, Guy reported that:

-----the gentleman does not give me the idea of a proposal
of a straitforward man.

The net result of Rowell's proposal was that his Syndicate partners would own 68.75 percent of the share capital, and Richard and Sir Edmund would have 31.25 percent, thus losing a controlling interest.

By October Rowell had revised his offer to give Richard Stephens and Sir Edmund Elton over 33.3 percent of the shares and was claiming that he deserved the higher share as he had put three months hard work into raising the Syndicate. This notwithstanding the efforts over several years of the inventors! In a letter to Sir Edmund Guy Kindersley said:

I am sorry that the fish are not up----after spending so much time
waiting for it.

Fortunately Richard Stephens had remembered his experience with Charles Audrey in 1899 and had sensed the way the fish were running and put in place alternative plans. In July 1907 he had obtained quotations for manufacture locally and was quoted five shillings per lighter by a Mr Evered. As the intention was to charge the Gas Company £1 0s per lighter this represented a good return. However the Clevedon Council were no pushover and the Chief Engineer of the Gas Company, J Harger Pye, wrote to Richard on August 10th 1908 to advise him that, despite his endeavours and the clear financial advantages, the Council had decided against wholesale adoption for the current year.

In August Mr Harger Pye wrote to Sir Edmund to say that the experience over the previous three years with the 'Pressure Lighters' had been very good. They were more reliable than the clock-operated lighters and as the control was in the hands of the Gas Works manager, they could be switched to suit weather and daylight conditions. They

Plate 7.3   *Clevedon Triangle and the Weston, Clevedon and*
Portishead Railway

123

also offered strong competition to the evolving electric lights for the same reason. Mr Pye said that he had no difficulty in recommending the lighters for wholesale installation in Clevedon.

Over the 1909-1910 winter the lighters were installed in Elton Road and Chapel Hill Clevedon. On 9th of June 1910 Mr Pye wrote to Sir Edmund to report that over the six months of installation the lighters had worked with a failure rate of only 1.1 percent which compared very favourably with the clock-driven lighters. He was particularly impressed by the fact that the regular maintenance man was off work due to illness and that his replacement had no difficulty in picking up the work.

In another letter dated the same day he expresses the wish that the Urban Council should place a five-year contract to fit up the whole of Clevedon with these lights. It seems probable that Mr Pye was sending these letters as recommendations to send to third parties, because Richard Stephens and Sir Edmund had taken out patents for the lighters in several other countries and no doubt needed references. Nevertheless the lighters were installed widely in Clevedon and gave good service for many years. Unfortunately they deprived the local lamplighter of his job.

1907 was a time of great change for Clevedon, when the Weston-super-Mare, Clevedon and Portishead railway was built. The existing branch line from Yatton terminated on Station Road opposite the Constitution Club, but the new railway cut right across the southern end of the Triangle, a few yards from Richard Stephens' works. (Colour Plate C20). A photograph taken in the early 1920s after Stephens had left Clevedon, shows the railway. Stephens' old works is on the right with a Raleigh bicycle advertisement on the end wall. Construction must have caused a lot of disruption and once it went into operation, whenever a train approached, it stopped all traffic. The trains had to slow to four mph and be preceded by a man carrying a red flag. (Plate 7.3).

The man with the sack trolley in the photograph is 'Fishy' Knight who used to own a fish and chip shop opposite the Waggon and Horses public house in Clevedon. He is still remembered by several Clevedon residents. Roger Triggol who owns a farm in Tickenham just outside Clevedon also remembers the engine driver, John Hedger, as Roger used to go to school with his son Mike. A popular story in Clevedon is of the occasion when another of the train drivers, Mr Cole, was attending a wedding reception and was asked whether he wasn't supposed to be on duty driving the train. "Oh yes" he said, munching into another corned beef sandwich, "I've parked it up in the town centre. Bugger the train!"

Roger Triggol keeps a fleet of classic cars which he hires out for weddings and other functions. He has five Austins from the 1920s and

124

Plate 7.4   Stephens Family 1906

Plate 7.5

1 and 2   Grandad and Granny Blackmore.   3 Mary Stephens

4. 5 and 6 Ada, Harold and Madge Tarrant.

7 to 12,   Cecilia and Phillip Day, with children, Percy in arms,

and Dick, Dolly and Phillip jnr standing in front.

13 Ewart, 14 Dick, 15 Percy.   16 and 17, Ethel and Ted Winter.

30s, but also has a beautiful 1921 Model T Ford Tourer and a Ford T Truck. He has an American Nash 691 and several other vehicles and tractors. An International Titan tractor in his possession has a belt drive and he advises that from time to time it requires the 'dirt on the belt' treatment, just like the belt-driven Stephens cars! The arrival of the rail link from Portishead made Richard Stephens' hackney carriage link from Clevedon redundant overnight. With his family now virtually fully grown up he determined to concentrate on his local taxi business and his motor servicing works.

Richard and Mary's family was now growing fast. Mary's father had died and her mother Sarah had re-married at the age of seventy. She and her husband, William Blackmore, visited the Stephens family at Clevedon in about 1906 and sat with the family for a portrait. Plate 7.4 shows the family members and Plate 7.5 is a key to their names. All six Stephens children are present together with a good collection of grand-children. The three girls were by now married. Ethel and Ted Winter were living next door to Richard at Number 9, The Triangle, whilst the eldest, Cecilia had married Phillip Day and at the time of the photograph their family of four children was complete.

Ada, married to Harold Tarrant, now had a daughter Madge. A few years later they had an opportunity to make a new life in America and moved from Weston-super-Mare to Chicago in Illinois with their children Madge and Harry. The Boulevard Congregational Church gave Ada a magnificent send-off party and eulogies were reported in the local newspaper. Mrs Hunt said that her singing had been a joy and inspiration to thousands of people who had visited the church and that, like her mother, she possessed a sweet voice, and he hoped she would make use of it in the new country. Ewart was working full-time with Richard who now named his business
Richard Stephens and Sons, Motor and General Engineers.

Percy was nineteen and whilst he was working in his father's business, was increasingly feeling a calling to follow a life of Evangelism in the Church. Dick was also working with his father but when he got engaged to a London girl he started to think about setting up his own engineering business.

Richard considered the time was ripe to update his fleet. The decade since he first started to build his cars had seen many advances. Solid tyres were now the exception and all new cars were fitted with pneumatic tyres. Also steering wheels had become fairly universal and drivers expected more comfort with enclosed cabins or convertible tops. Richard therefore progressively sold off most of his fleet during 1907 and 1908. He kept AE 174 for his own use. However in about 1908 he cut up the hackney carriage AE 341 with a hacksaw and donated the engine to the Science Museum. The rest of the body was packed into tea chests by Dick. Some other cars were cut up and mainly scrapped, although some parts, including an engine, were also kept. Richard used the proceeds of the sale of his fleet together with his now considerable savings to set about purchasing a brand new fleet of Model T Fords.

Chapter 8
Fords and Family

In about 1900 Henry Ford, an American engineer, visited England for a short time. He was intent on setting up his own car manufacturing company and was keen to see what was happening in Europe where car design and manufacturing was progressing rapidly. A friend of Thomas Edison, he had almost certainly heard about Richard Stephens. It is a Stephens family tradition, and a very likely one, that Ford visited Richard Stephens and saw his cars.

Henry Ford (Plate 8.1), was born July 30, 1863, on his family's farm in Dearborn, Michigan. From the time he was a young boy, he enjoyed tinkering with machinery. His work on the farm and a job in a Detroit machine shop meant that he was well versed in engineering and able to experiment with his ideas at will. In 1891 he became a part-time engineer with the Edison Illuminating Company and he and Thomas Edison remained close friends for decades.

In his spare time Ford tinkered with creating a motorized vehicle, and in 1896 introduced his 'Quadricycle', a four-wheeled buggy-type vehicle with a gasoline engine. (Plate 8.2). He sold this in order to finance work on an improved vehicle. With the financial backing of the mayor of Detroit, Ford built a second experimental car in 1899. It was larger, sturdier, and heavier than the 'Quadricycle'. After Ford had driven it to Pontiac, Michigan and back without incident, William H. Murphy, a wealthy Detroit lumber merchant, agreed to help Ford form a company to manufacture motorcars.

In August 1899 the Detroit Automobile Company was formed but Ford put up no money for his shares of stock. Ten days later he resigned from his part-time position at Edison to become superintendent in charge of production at the Detroit Automobile Company, at a monthly salary of $150. The Detroit Automobile Company went out of business in November 1900 after turning out only about a dozen automobiles. It was then that Ford decided on his visit to Europe. On his trip to England Ford travelled to Manchester to visit the Crossley brothers who had been producing vehicle engines for several years.

Francis (Frank) and William (later Sir William) Crossley were two brothers who had served their apprenticeships at two great Newcastle engineering companies, being Robert Stephenson and W G Armstrong,

Plate 8.1   Henry Ford

respectively. In 1867 they set up in partnership as Crossley Brothers. Frank had bought the engineering business of John M. Dunlop at Great Marlborough Street in Manchester with financial assistance from his uncle. Dunlop manufactured pumps, presses and small steam engines.

The Crossley brothers were strictly teetotal and whilst they did not refrain from taking orders from breweries, they refused to solicit them,

Plate 8.2   Henry Ford and his 1896 Quadricycle

and any profits accruing from such sales were given to charitable organisations. They adopted the early Christian Coptic Cross as the badge for their road vehicles. In 1881 Crossley Brothers became a limited company and in 1882 as their business grew, they moved to larger premises in Pottery Lane, Openshaw, in East Manchester. In 1869 they purchased the worldwide patent rights of Nicolaus Otto and Eugen Langen of Cologne for the new gas-fuelled atmospheric internal combustion engine. (In this arrangement the expanding hot gas blows the piston upwards before being exhausted. It is the atmospheric pressure combined with the weight of the piston that then forces the piston down, driving the flywheel round, via a ratchet.) In 1876 these rights were extended to the famous Otto four stroke cycle engine. Considering that Otto had only patented his engine in 1861 this was a remarkably prescient move, but the inventors did retain their rights in Germany. The change over to four stroke engines was remarkably rapid, as the first one was built in 1876, and the last atmospheric engines were made in 1877!

Whilst the introduction of the carburettor allowed much more volatile

Plate 8.3   Henry Ford and the 1903 Model 'A'

hydrocarbons to be used with hot tube or spark ignition, the Crossley brothers concentrated on developing the heavy oil engine with the first one being demonstrated in 1891. In 1896 they obtained rights to the Diesel system which did not require spark ignition. After Frank died in 1897, the company did produce some petrol engines and in the early 1900s supplied some of these for Leyland buses.

The Crossley company was amongst the first to introduce a continuous production line, with its huge advantages in manufacturing efficiency. This was a static line with the workforce adding components as they went along the line. According to Eyre, Heaps and Townsin in their definitive book on Crossley Motors, Henry Ford visited the company at Pottery Lane at the turn of the century and was probably heavily influenced by what he saw. On his return to Michigan in 1901 he set up the Henry Ford Company, where he insisted on being employed as the engineer, this being his *forte.* In a dispute with his financiers he resigned and in 1903 set up another company, the Ford Motor Company. Meanwhile the Henry Ford Company became the Cadillac Motor Car Company.

In 1903 Ford launched his first popular car, the single-cylinder Model A, (Plate 8.3), and this was manufactured on a fixed production line, just like that which he had witnessed at Crossley Brothers. Later in that year two Model A cars were imported into England and in March 1904 they were displayed at the Cordingley Automobile show in Islington, London. As a result, Aubrey Blakiston set up an agency in Long Acre, London. The following year a number of four-cylinder Model B Fords were imported but these did not sell immediately and three were later fitted with landaulet bodies for taxi use. It is likely that John Hunt of Bath heard of these cars and ordered his own taxis from the agency.

The Model A car was followed by a succession of lettered models, the other four-cylinder examples being the N, R, and S. Ford had the vision to see that the motor car was the key to the future development of society. The wide States of Michigan and Illinois with their huge farms and hundreds of miles of open country were largely inaccessible to the general populace. Even the farming communities were cut off and the railroad connections were few and far between. Ford saw that giving each farmer a reliable, cheap car would open up a big market.

With the Models N, R and S, which differed only in detail, Henry Ford was getting close to what he wished to achieve, but being basically two-seaters (with an optional rear third seat) and an 84-inch wheelbase they did not adequately provide for family motoring (Plate 8.4). He therefore set about improving the design to overcome this shortcoming. In 1906 Ford had purchased a four-cylinder engine from the Crossley company, no doubt to see how he might improve his own engines. By early 1908 he had created his most famous motorcar: the Model T Ford

News of the new four-cylinder, four-seater model travelled fast and Richard Stephens was ready to invest in the new technology. His brother Davey in the United States kept him informed of the progress of the motor industry and visited Richard in 1907.

At the British Olympia Motor Exhibition in November 1907 the Ford stand showed a mixture of cars, including two Model Ns with a wheelbase extended to 93 inches, stronger axles and springs, and both fitted with a four-seater bodies, one a double-phaeton and the other a landaulet. These were the precursors of the forthcoming Model T with its 100-inch wheelbase. It is likely that Richard Stephens attended this exhibition with Davey, who returned to the USA in the December.

Production of the Model T started in October 1908 and the car was an immediate success. The production line technique enabled a complete car to be produced every 728 minutes (about twelve hours), a huge improvement over most other car manufacturers where vehicles were virtually hand-made. (In 1914 a car rolled off the production line every 93 minutes, but by this time Ford had developed the rolling production

132

Plate 8.4   Ford Model 'S', 1907

line, in which the cars travel slowly along a conveyor belt and the workforce stays in the same location).

Henry Ford was desperate to have the Model T ready for the European motor exhibition season of the late autumn and up to six of the first cars off the production line were immediately shipped to London for display at the Olympia Exhibition in November 1908. Some, but not all, of these cars were then shipped to Paris for the Exhibition there in January 1909. The history of the early vehicles is somewhat confused as modifications were being introduced all the time, but it is possible that some of this early batch went to Richard Stephens.

Whatever the exact timing, within a year Richard had taken delivery, and he commenced a new taxi and car hire service. He transferred the registration plate across from the original hackney carriage to one of the Fords, (Plate 8.5), and a brochure from 1911 shows how his taxi service was flourishing using the Model Ts. (Colour Plate C21).

Dick and Ewart continued in the business and Dick got married in 1908 and set up home at 4 Park Road in Clevedon with his wife Lily Mary Maud. In 1910 they moved to Wandsworth where Dick set about starting up a South London branch of Richard Stephens and Sons. Arch Binding had gone to work at the Straker Squire car factory in Bristol, but his younger brother William Percy was driving for Richard Stephens.

Plate 8.5   Richard Stephens' First Model 'T' Ford Taxi

Plate 8.9   Engine Stands for the MOD

A small boy is demonstrating how easy it was to handle the engine. The frames folded flat to ease storage and sold for £3 18s 6d.

Just after war did eventually break out, in September 1914, Ewart and Arch Binding replied to an advertisement by the Royal Naval Air Service asking for volunteers. (Plate 8.11). Ewart served as an engineering mechanic with the rank of Flight Sergeant, eventually rising to Petty Officer. (Colour Plate C23). He served at Hornsea in the East Riding of Yorkshire with 79th Wing and was transferred to the Royal Air Force when it was created from the merger of the Royal Flying Corps and the Royal Naval Air Service in 1917.

Arch served on airships, rising to the rank of Warrant Officer before also transferring into the RAF. He received an award of twelve pounds ten shillings for designing a carburettor that ran on hydrogen. Until then airships had to land to re-fuel, or hover over a ship whilst fuel was transferred aboard, a very hazardous activity. With the new carburettor, hydrogen from the gas bag could be used as fuel, a virtually inexhaustible supply.

Arch was also awarded the Air Force Cross for bravery. This was for climbing out of an airship gondola to replace the magnetos on both engines. Before 1914 British aircraft engines all used Bosch magnetos, which were very reliable, but the supply dried up at the outbreak of war. Replacement magnetos built in the UK were far less reliable. The Air

139

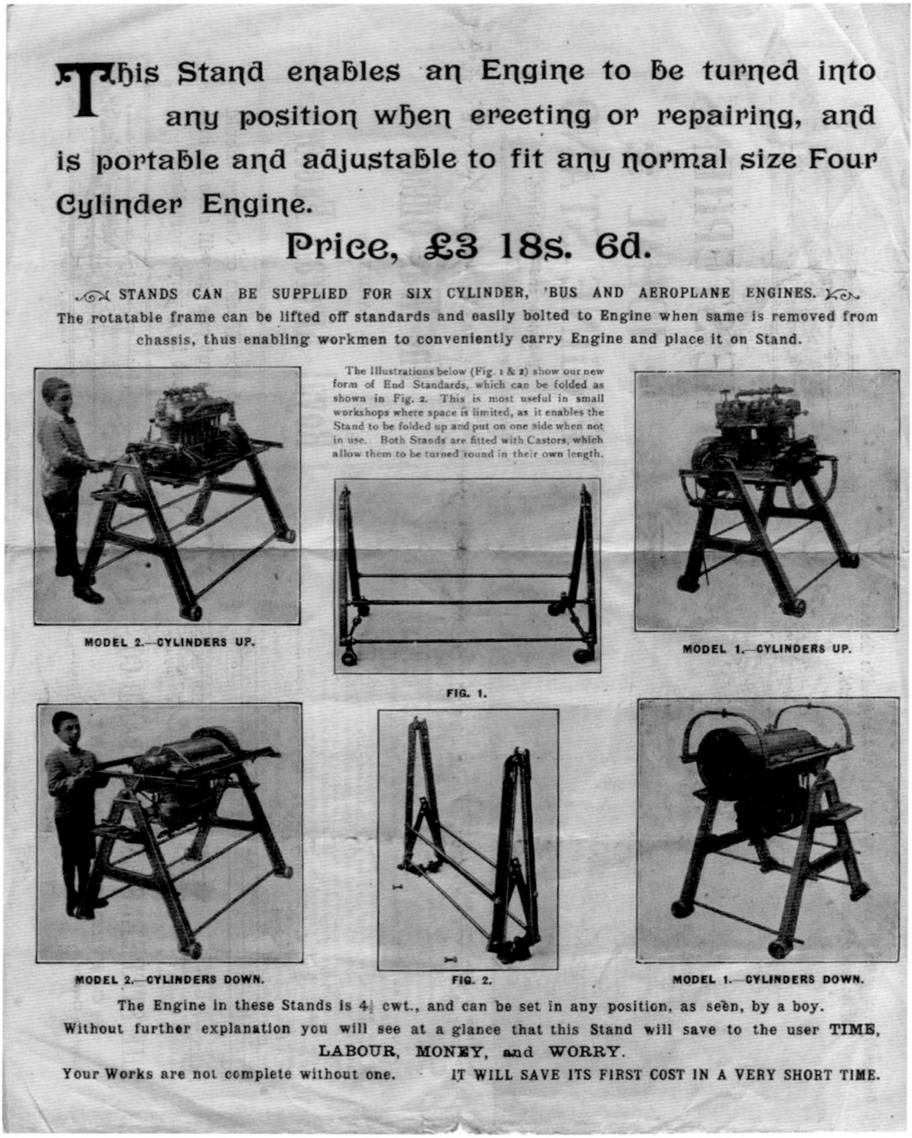

This Stand enables an Engine to be turned into any position when erecting or repairing, and is portable and adjustable to fit any normal size Four Cylinder Engine.

Price, £3 18s. 6d.

STANDS CAN BE SUPPLIED FOR SIX CYLINDER, 'BUS AND AEROPLANE ENGINES.

The rotatable frame can be lifted off standards and easily bolted to Engine when same is removed from chassis, thus enabling workmen to conveniently carry Engine and place it on Stand.

The Illustrations below (Fig. 1 & 2) show our new form of End Standards, which can be folded as shown in Fig. 2. This is most useful in small workshops where space is limited, as it enables the Stand to be folded up and put on one side when not in use. Both Stands are fitted with Castors, which allow them to be turned round in their own length.

MODEL 2.—CYLINDERS UP.

MODEL 1.—CYLINDERS UP.

FIG. 1.

MODEL 2.—CYLINDERS DOWN.

FIG. 2.

MODEL 1.—CYLINDERS DOWN.

The Engine in these Stands is 4½ cwt., and can be set in any position, as seen, by a boy.

Without further explanation you will see at a glance that this Stand will save to the user **TIME, LABOUR, MONEY, and WORRY.**

Your Works are not complete without one.   IT WILL SAVE ITS FIRST COST IN A VERY SHORT TIME.

Plate 8.10   Engine Stand Brochure

Ministry made it a requirement for all aero engines to be fitted with duplicate magnetos but it was not at all unusual for both to fail on a long flight, so it was essential to carry on board a stock of spares.

During the war Ewart still maintained a close interest in the business. With the war and its casualties uppermost in everyone's minds, in 1916 he and his father patented folding stretchers for ambulances, which

140

Plate 8.11   Arch Binding and Ewart Stephens in RNAS Uniform

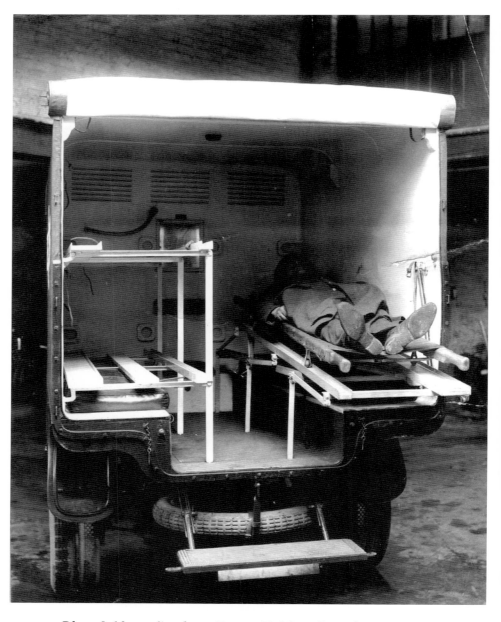

Plate 8.12   Stephens Patent Folding Stretcher Carrier

enabled casualties to be loaded into the ambulance with the minimum of discomfort and enabled the stretchers to be folded sideways when out of use, for the transportation of field personnel. The first set was sold to 'Jacko', a local ambulance operator. (Plate 8.12).

142

Chapter 9
Growth and Decline

Richard continued to develop his ideas and in 1917 he and Ewart patented the *Stephens Adjustable Drum Brake with Internal Shoes*. This was the development for cars of the calliper brake which he had invented for bicycles. It automatically balanced the pressure on the brake drums whilst having a simple adjuster to take up slack caused by wear. This was done by means of a tapered wedge, a technique which is now used universally.

During the war the family members had disseminated and made their own ways in life. Cecilia had moved with her family to Southampton. Dick moved with Lily and their two children Richard and Audrey from Wandsworth to 63 Church Road Upper Norwood. In a factory at No. 115 Church Road, Dick opened up a London branch of the business, 'Richard Stephens and Sons Ltd, Engineering, Gauge and Tool Makers'. He took with him the parts of the Stephens prototype car AE 341 still in its tea chests, minus the engine.

In about 1915 Percy had married Anne Badenoch and they went to live in Oak Park, a suburb of Chicago. In 1917 their twins, Richard and Clemence were born. Percy was still earning a living from motor engineering, but pursued his real vocation of being an evangelical preacher. He was a Christian Scientist and in the same year he lectured in Chicago on the subject of *Christian Science: its Pedigree, Principles and Posterity.* A number of pamphlets from this time show that he had a considerable following. When America entered the First World War in 1917 he was Pastor of the Second Baptist Church in Chicago. Percy was assessed by the Draft Board and declared medically fit but the Board must have considered that his engineering work and evangelical activities were too important for him to be drafted, so he remained a civilian. He did contribute to the war effort however by running a series of 'Evangelistic Sermons' in what was called The World War Series. (Plate 9.1).

Ewart was discharged from the RAF in October 1918 and, still unmarried, went back to the family house in Clevedon where he helped his father manufacture the brake shoes which were starting to sell rather well. He also dabbled in shares and earned something of a living from the stock market.

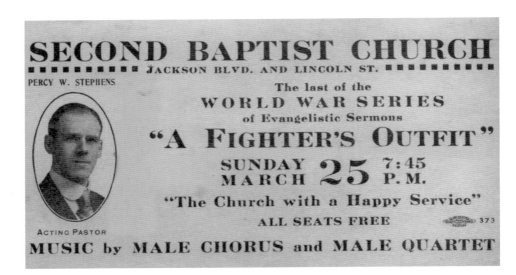

Plate 9.1   Percy Stephens Sermon Series for the World War

Richard continued with his taxi and motor engineering work all during the First World War but was finding that demand for his patented brake shoes was outstripping his capacity to supply. He had obtained a large contract with a Ford dealer to supply the shoes for the Model T cars and One Ton trucks.

Richard decided to concentrate the business in the London works so he and Mary sold the Clevedon motor business in 1919 as a going concern and moved from Clevedon. They did so with great regret, for they had many friends in the town. His colleague and mentor Sir Edmund Elton was in poor health, suffering from the effects of lead poisoning due to the glazes he used for his pottery. He died in 1920 and his son Ambrose tried to continue the work but Richard's brother-in-law George Masters, who threw the pots, died shortly afterwards and so the pottery was closed.

Ted Winter, Richard's son-in-law owned a long lease to a property, 'Coniston', close to the Upper Norwood works on Fox Hill just off Church Road and close to Dick's house. Ted sub-let the lease to Richard and so he, Mary and Ewart moved there.

Richard and the two sons continued the business, manufacturing and selling the brake shoes that they had patented. Richard did however continue to own and visit the properties in Clevedon and enjoyed a good income from leasing them. After the war Arch Binding, who had been Richard's chief mechanic, joined with Harry Payne to set up their own business on Old Church Road in Clevedon, which expanded to Yeovil

144

and survived for many years until Arch's retirement.

A photograph from about this time shows Richard and Mary Stephens elegantly dressed and sitting comfortably posed on a bench in front of a landscape scene. (Colour Plate C24). They enjoyed their new situation and took breaks in the south coast towns of Brighton and Hove.

With the growing success of the brake shoe business Richard had protected his interests by extending the patent to America, and he opened up agencies in Durban South Africa, Brisbane Australia, Gentilly France and of course in Chicago Illinois. Percy was to leave his motor engineering employers and manage the American company whilst still carrying on his pastoral duties at the Chicago Second Baptist Church.

A family conference was convened and in 1920 Percy and his family travelled to England to visit Richard and Mary and to plan how to organise the growing business. Ewart still had the prototype Stephens car and Percy took the opportunity to renew his acquaintance with it. He drove it around the streets of Upper Norwood and he, Ann, and their children Richard and Clemence were photographed in it. (Plate 9.2).

Richard, Ewart, Percy and Dick set about creating their company to market the brake shoes worldwide. They arranged a photo-shoot at Leigh Hill in South London and invited the trade press. For the photo-shoot the prototype car was re-fitted with its original spoked wheels and fitted with publicity placards. Articles duly appeared in several trade journals with a rare photograph of the four men together. (Plate 9.3).

They were described by their company titles as follows –

Mr A E Stephens – Production Manager of R Stephens and Sons, General Superintendent of Factories in London and Paris, Member of the British Motor Manufacturers Association;

Mr P W Stephens – President of R Stephens Co, General Manager Chicago Factory and of American Distribution, Inventor of Gasignal;

Mr R J Stephens – Formerly President of Humphries-Stephens Motor Co, Member of the British Motor Manufacturers Association, Manager of European Business of R Stephens and Sons London and Paris;

Mr R Stephens – Inventor of the Original Stephens Motor Car, also inventor of Stephens Snow Plough, Stephens Automatic Lighter, Stephens Dress Clip, Stephens Adjustable Brake Shoe, etc.

Plate 9.2   Percy, Anne, Clemence and Richard Stephens, 1920

Percy returned to Chicago shortly afterwards to set up the agency. By 1924 the brake shoes were being marketed in America by the General Asbestos and Rubber Company as the *Garco-Stephens Adjustable Brake Shoe for Cars and Trucks*. His visit appears to have inspired a spate of motor car innovation. In June of 1921 and again in November Ewart travelled to America to visit Percy. In 1921 Percy was granted a USA patent for a vehicle fuel reserve indicator and tank, the Gasignal. Later he filed another similar patent and in 1927 he patented an auxiliary air intake device to stop motor car engines from overheating. Percy's motor engineering career seems to have come to an end in about 1927 when he became an engineer for a kitchen equipment manufacturer, the Cast-Rite Corporation. Between 1929 and 1942 he took out eleven patents for kitchen equipment, including juice extractors and various improvements to pressure cookers.

Ada and Harold, also living in Chicago, retired to Florida in the 1930s and lived in Daytona Beach. Whilst they had two children Harry and Madge, both of these were childless. Harry became an airline pilot and in 1933 on Mothers' Day he presented Ada with a cake in the shape of

146

Plate 9.3   Ewart, Percy, Dick and Richard Stephens in 1920

147

Plate 9.4   Ada and Harry Tarrant. Mothers' Day 1933

an aeroplane decorated with feathers. (Plate 9.4). Later that same year he was killed in an aeroplane crash in Michigan. The cause of the crash was not fully explained but it seems likely that one of the passengers had boarded with an inflammable cargo and that it had ignited.

Richard's second daughter Cecilia and her husband Phillip had four children, Phillip, Dick, Percy and Cecilia, called Dolly. Ethel and Ted Winter ran a jewellery shop for several years on Clevedon Triangle.

Plate 9.5   The Stephens Norwood Workshop in 1923

They emigrated to South Africa to live in Port Elizabeth but did not have any children.

The brake shoes business flourished (Plate 9.5), with the company also supplying brakes for Ford vehicles to another company, Baico Patents Ltd. Baico specialised in providing chassis extensions, and they supplied conversion kits for the Ford one ton truck the *Tonner*, which extended the chassis to give a two-and-a-half ton capability. This enabled them to be used for fire engines and charabancs and similar vehicles. The improved brake shoes were just what such vehicles required to cope with the heavier loads. Richard advertised the brake shoes widely and the application to Fords was prominent in his literature. The shoes cost thirty-five shillings for a set for a car and fifty-two shillings and sixpence for a lorry set. (Colour Plate C25).

Richard had a stand in the Palace of Engineering at the British Empire Exhibition in 1924. The exhibition had been planned at the end of the First World War and was on the site of playing fields at Wembley. The architects Sir John Simpson and Maxwell Ayrton were commissioned to

149

Plate 9.6   Stephens Stand at the British Empire Exhibition

design a vast stadium which would be retained after the exhibition for sports events. At a cost of seven hundred and fifty thousand pounds it took just three hundred days to complete and was the largest concrete structure in the world. Amongst other displays in the Palace of Engineering was the famous 'Flying Scotsman' locomotive.

The exhibition was opened on St George's Day, 23rd April, 1924 by King George V. The Stephens stand was number 110 and displayed sets of brake shoes for cars and trucks. Richard was also apparently intent on further expansion because the stand also had a plaque requesting offers of interest for overseas agencies. (Plate 9.6).

The success at the British Empire Exhibition was overshadowed for the family by a sad event. It was on one of their stays in Brighton that Mary Stephens passed away in May 1924. Tributes in the Brighton, Norwood and Clevedon newspapers all praised her gentle and devout ways. She had travelled the world in her youth, raised a family of six children and fed and boarded Richard's apprentices during the early years in Clevedon. She had taken in her niece Jessie to help her sister Elizabeth after John Stacey had died, looked after some of her grandchildren, run Bible Classes in Clevedon and sung in the church choir in Weston-super-Mare.

The following month Percy came back to England on the *Berengaria* to visit the family and pay his respects on his mother's passing. He returned home later that month on the *Aquitania*. In June of the following year Dick and his wife Lily travelled on the *Aquitania* to the USA, to pay a return visit to Percy and his wife Anne.

Shortly afterwards Richard took the decision to fully retire and live permanently on the South Coast. He moved to Derek Avenue in Hove, Sussex and Ewart, who was still unmarried, went with him, leaving Dick to manage the Upper Norwood business. Richard and Ewart became keen members of the Brighton and Hove Bowling Club and there Richard met a Miss Florence Steane. Florence, who had recently retired to the area due to ill health, was the former headmistress of Grange Street Girls School in Burton-on-Trent and was an accomplished musician. She composed a number of pieces which were published and was very popular with the girls under her care, particularly as she organised musical entertainments with them.

Richard and Florence were married in the spring of 1925 in Steyning, West Sussex. They made a visit to Chicago to see Percy and his family in September 1926 and stayed for a couple of months, returning on the *Berengaria.*

Now that he was retired, Richard started to take more interest in other aspects of historical motoring. Amongst other things he was a founder member of the Circle of Ninteenth Century Motorists. This was the the very small and elite group of people who had owned or driven cars before the conclusion of the 1900 Thousand Miles Trial of the ACGB&I. (Automobile Club of Great Britain and Ireland).

The Automobile Club of Great Britain was formed in 1897, and Ireland was included shortly afterwards as an afterthought. The original objective of the club was that it should be:

a society for the encouragement of automobilism.

Whilst not explicitly stated it was really a very upper class club. In 1901 the Club formed the Motor Union so:

that all automobilists without reference to the question of social position----should be embodied under one banner.

In March 1907 Royal patronage was bestowed upon the Club and it became the Royal Automobile Club.

The Motor Union, increasingly uncomfortable with the elitism still prevalent in the Club, then left the RAC in 1908 to be absorbed by the Automobile Association (AA) in 1910.

The Circle of Nineteenth Century Motorists was founded in November 1927 and at one time its membership reached 220. The main objective of the Circle was to hold annual reunions, the first being on 14th of December 1927 at the Piccadilly Hotel. It is not clear how much the Royal Automobile Club was involved in or responsible for the Circle. At the time it would have been difficult for any committed motorist who had driven prior to the twentieth century to not also have been a member of the Royal Automobile Club. The RAC does keep the Circle's archives and in 1966 the surviving members presented the Club with a board, listing all the Presidents and Chairmen, (including Dick Stephens), which now hangs in the Pall Mall clubhouse.

The founding of the Circle arose directly from a veteran car journey instigated by The *Daily Sketch* and *Sunday Graphic* in November 1927. This was from London to Brighton, and was to commemorate the 1896 'Emancipation' run. It commenced with a trip from their offices to the Olympia Motor Exhibition and thousands crowded the streets to view the spectacle. The run was open to all cars constructed before 1904. Richard and Ewart duly entered the prototype car AE 174 and it was highly commended, winning a Gold Medal.

Colour Plate C26 shows the medal with on the obverse, a picture of the car and a clearly recognisable Richard Stephens driving. A scantily-Clad figure rides on the rear flourishing a sash carrying the word

'Emancipation!' On the reverse is stamped:

Awarded by the Daily Sketch and Sunday Graphic to R Stephens and Sons

and the legend around the perimeter says:

Old Crocks Emancipation Day Parade Nov. 13. 1927

Plate 9.7   Richard and Ewart Stephens on the 1927 Run to Olympia.

Plate 9.7 shows Richard and Ewart in the car on the preliminary trip to from the *Daily Sketch* offices to Olympia. The car is carrying a contemporary number plate, RK 7076.

The following year Richard and Ewart drove the car in a repeat of this London to Brighton Run and completed it at an average speed of 19.3 mph. (Plate 9.8). In later years the car made the London to Brighton run many times.

Between November 1928 and January 1929 a quixotic exchange took place between Dick, father Richard and the Circle of Nineteenth Century Motorists. Dick, who had first started driving the prototype Stephens car in 1898 at the age of thirteen and a half, applied for membership of the Circle. The application was rejected and Dick protested, giving further details of his experience and also stating that John Hunt, whom Dick had taught to drive in 1900 and was still alive, could verify the accuracy of the application.

A few days later Richard, who was already a founder member of the Circle, also wrote to the Secretary giving his support. (Colour Plate 27). Dick's membership was rapidly granted and he went on to be Chairman of the Circle in later years.

GOLD MEDALLIST
Old Crocks Run—London to Brighton, 52 m.
Nov. 18th, 1928. Speed 19.3 m.p.h.
THE FIRST ENTIRELY BRITISH CAR.

*Plate 9.8   Richard and Ewart Stephens in the 1928
London to Brighton Run*

At some time just after this a serious rift took place between Dick and the rest of the family. The cause is not known and may have concerned the contents of Richard's will following his re-marriage, but Richard did not allow any members of his family to speak to Dick thereafter. Dick moved home at about this time to an adjacent street. His new address was *Madoc,* 155 Adelaide Road, Upper Norwood, named after his place of birth. Dick still continued with the Upper Norwood works but he removed the letter 'S' from the name board over the entrance so that it read 'Stephens and Son Ltd'. This would imply that the partnership with his father and brothers had broken up. As his own son was a solicitor in Reading it is difficult to see what part he actually played in the business.

Richard Stephens and Ewart took AE 174 on several further trips including the London to Brighton Runs and the London to Eastbourne Run in 1931. Plate 9.9 shows them both at the end of the latter journey which they completed in fifteenth place at a speed of 15.48 mph, a very creditable average.

Later in 1931 the car suffered an accident in which the back main

Plate 9.9   Richard and Ewart finish the
1931 London to Eastbourne Run

tube of the frame was broken. Owing to the considerable amount of work involved in fitting a new tube the old one was brazed up in situ. Unfortunately it was slightly off-centre with the result that the extension shaft carrying the driving pulleys was subjected to considerable flexing.

Richard Stephens died on Sunday 31st January 1932 at his home in Hove. He was seventy-five and had suffered a short bout of influenza and bronchitis about three weeks previously. He had seemed to improve but took a sudden turn for the worse and peacefully passed away.

Tributes poured in from all parts of the motoring fraternity and obituaries were published in Hove, Lewisham and Clevedon. He was especially remembered for his pioneering motor works in Clevedon. Whilst there will always be disputes over priority, none doubt that he was the original inventor of his cars, their engines and equipment, or that these were the first all-British cars with independent front suspension to go into series production.

Epilogue

Richard Stephens may have had died but his cars lived on. Ewart Stephens continued to drive the prototype car and it was entered in a number of rallies and runs. The engine of the Bath hackney carriage AE 341 was still in the Science Museum and Dick had the rest of the car stored away in tea chests.

Ewart inherited the bulk of his father's possessions. He exercised an option to buy the lease of 'Coniston' in Upper Norwood from Ted Winter and he let it out to tenants. He continued to lease out the properties in Clevedon and visited there regularly. Roger Triggol remembers his visits and says that around Clevedon he was always known as 'Steve.'

Ewart married Gwendoline Lamb in 1934 at Herne Hill in London and they took a long honeymoon, travelling virtually around the world. (Plate E1). Their daughter Georgina was born in 1935. (Plate E2). The family moved home several times in the Sussex area but Ewart continued to rally the prototype car.

In September 1937 Ada and Harold visited from Florida and went to Weston-super-Mare and Clevedon to visit old friends. On the way she called in to see Charles Redrup who was living in Clifton, Bristol, where he was working on his wobble-plate engine for the Bristol Tramways and Carriage Company. When Ada went to see Dick, she gave him Charles' address, and Dick called in to see Charles in Bristol in the December. They had a merry time reminiscing about the early cars and Charles was amazed to hear that the prototype car was still going strong.

During the middle of the Second World War in August 1942 Percy Stephens passed away at his home in Chicago. He was only 55 but much respected in the Baptist Church community in Chicago.

Ewart drove the prototype in the 'Brooklands Old Crocks Race' in August 1939 just prior to the outbreak of war. This was the last car race meet at Brooklands because after the war the banked track was considered too dangerous for the speeds that cars could then attain. The car was was laid up during the war and Ewart only brought it out again in 1944 after D-day. In Plate E3 Georgina is seen with a friend in the car which is still bearing the Brooklands race plate.

A little while after the end of the Second World War in 1947 Ewart and Gwen decided to emigrate to South Africa where Ethel and Ted Winter were living in Port Elizabeth. They sold up all their properties

Plate E1   Wedding of Ewart Stephens and Gwendoline Lamb

and made the travel arrangements. Ewart sold AE 174 to Arch Binding whose garage business of Binding and Payne Ltd was thriving in Yeovil and Clevedon.   At the last moment Ewart got cold feet, probably due to

Plate E2   *Ewart, Gwen and Georgina*

health concerns. He and Gwen together with daughter Georgina had to start afresh and moved into temporary accommodation before eventually settling again in Hove.

Sometime later Arch Binding sold AE 174 to Dick Stephens who continued to rally it. It was entered in the Dorking Hill Speed climb in 1951 and completed the task in 142.1 seconds. On the third of June in the same year the car was entered in a run from Hyde Park to Windsor.

It went on yet another run on the ninth of June, this time from Birmingham to Coventry. When the cars were lined up at the start, Dick's car was just behind a Daimler that had belonged to Edward VII. The event was due to be initiated by the then Princess Elizabeth and before the start she went to look at the Daimler. To Dick's surprise she was then brought to see him, as he was one of the original builders of the car. She asked about its age, how easy was it to drive, and had it been in the London to Brighton Run.

Plate E4 is a photograph taken at the time, with Dick facing the Princess. Dick's wife Lily is between them in the black hat with her back to the camera.

Just a month later on the 14th of July the car made a return to the West Country and ran in the Festival of Britain Car Run from Bristol to

158

Plate E3   Ewart, Georgina and Friend, Bournemouth, 1944

Weston-super-Mare and back.   Plate E5 shows Alderman T W R Proctor, Mayor of Weston-super-Mare greeting Dick on his arrival.

In Hyde Park at the start of the London to Brighton Run in November 1951 the crankshaft broke close to the flywheel and the car had to be scratched. The distorted back tube and the flexing pulley drive-shaft arising from the incident in 1931 had eventually taken their toll. However Dick now did a proper repair job, stripping the car down, replacing the faulty tube and fitting a new crankshaft. The car has run impeccably ever since.

Later that year AE 174 appeared in *The Magic Box*, the life story of the inventor of the cine camera, William Friese-Greene, (Colour Plate C28), and in 1953 it made a few brief appearances in the film *Genevieve*, with Dick driving. Colour Plate C29 shows Dick driving past a marshal who, unfortunately, is obscuring most of the car!

When Dick Stephens retired his engineering business was sold. The buildings lay derelict for many years and in 2006 were sold to a property development company for £440,000. No work has taken place since and the premises on Church Road Upper Norwood still carry the *Stephens and Son* name board. (Colour Plate C30).

The car was entered No. 1 in the 1955 London to Brighton Run with Dick driving and Lily as passenger. (Plate E6).

*Plate E4   Princess Elizabeth Views the Stephens
Prototype Car in June 1951*

*Plate E5   Arrival in Weston-Super-Mare during
The 1951 Festival Run from Bristol*

During Dick's chairmanship of the Circle of Nineteenth Century Motorists in 1960, he hosted the Duke of Edinburgh to the annual luncheon in the Pall Mall headquarters of the RAC. The average age of members there, which included George Lanchester, was eighty. (Plate E7, George Lanchester is between Dick Stephens and the Duke of Edinburgh)

More rallies followed after Dick's retirement and in 1960 the car was the first to arrive at the sea front in the London to Brighton Run. Dick rarely missed a year but he did miss the 1962 Run. On the 10th of May he was involved in an accident on the London to Eastbourne road. He was driving a Bentley and came up behind an eight-ton articulated lorry. As he started to overtake, the lorry in its turn pulled out to overtake a parked van near the top of a slight incline. As the vehicles came three abreast a Triumph Herald appeared over the hill coming the other way. Mrs Joan Spink, the driver of the Herald could not avoid a collision. Despite pleas from his Counsel about his exemplary sixty-year accident-free record, Dick was fined twenty-five pounds with twenty-one pounds fourteen shillings costs, and banned from driving for six months. He also had the indignity of having to take a driving test!

161

Plate E6   Dick and Lily Stephens in the
London to Brighton Run 1955

By the end of the 1960s Dick was an octogenarian and in 1969 he made his last drive in AE 174. At the age of eighty-four he drove in a veteran car rally from Bristol to Weston-super-Mare, with Arch Binding as his passenger. Shortly afterwards he put the car up for auction at Sothebys, together with the tea chests full of the parts of AE 341 and other cars. The two cars failed to meet their reserve price but AE 174 was later bought privately for two thousand six hundred pounds by Mr Robin Loder, proprietor of the Motor Museum at Leonardslee Gardens in Horsham, West Sussex.

Dick approached the Curator of the Science Museum and was able to persuade him to relinquish the Stephens engine of the 1900 hackney carriage, on the understanding that it was going to be re-instated in an operational vehicle. A few weeks later Robin Loder took his cheque book to Dick's home bought the parts of AE 341 and its engine, plus the parts of other vehicles from Dick.

Dick Stephens died in 1971 just before his eighty-sixth birthday. He requested that his ashes be scattered in the churchyard of All Saints in

Plate E7   Circle of Nineteenth Century Motorists Annual Dinner 1960
The Duke of Edinburgh (centre) Dick Stephens (left Foreground)

Clevedon, home of his formative years. His wife Lily aged eighty-six survived him and went to live in Scotland. She lived to be a hundred.

As well as being the youngest nineteenth century car driver and the youngest licenced hackney carriage driver, Dick had become a motor engineer and business man in his own right. He had stalwartly promoted his father's career and achievements and rallied his prototype car at every opportunity. He had been National Chairman of the 'Veteran Car Association' and one of the few surviving members of the ' Circle of Nineteenth Century Motorists'.

Similarly Ewart Stephens had worked from an early age with his father, not only on cars but also co-patenting the automatic gas lighters, ambulance stretchers and adjustable brake shoes. Whilst the prototype car had been in his possession he had regularly rallied it. After settling down again in Hove following the decision not to move abroad Ewart was semi-retired and made his living from the stock markets and property. His wife Gwen died in 1969 and he lived to be eighty-eight. He remarried shortly before his death in 1979.

His daughter Georgina was trained as an infant teacher and in April 1960 was married in Hove to Jack Westlake, a professional soldier. He

163

was in the Royal Corps of Signals, often working abroad, and they eventually returned to England where Jack retired with the rank of Brigadier. They now live in Forest Row, East Sussex where Georgina has an excellent archive of Richard Stephens' photographs and papers.

Robin Loder was of a similar mind to Dick and Ewart, believing that veteran cars should be seen and heard. With the tea-chests full of pieces of tubing, frames and assorted parts from the original Stephens hackney carriage and the case containing the engine from the Science Museum, he set about trying to re-assemble the car. When he opened the engine packing case he knew immediately that it was the right engine, for the hacksaw blade cuts across the engine mounts matched identically with the cuts on the car frames. Using sections of broom handle to locate the pieces together and with a lot of trial and error, he was eventually able to restore the hackney carriage to its former glory, although it took over ten years. (Colour Plate C15). The car was entered into the London to Brighton Run for the first time in 1981 and was the first car to arrive in Brighton.

As well as putting the two Stephens cars on display in his museum Robin Loder frequently rallied them. In 1996 Robin and Georgina Westlake rode AE 174 to second place in the London to Brighton Run. (Colour Plate C31).

Both cars took part in the 1995 London to Brighton run, the first time they had been entered together, and came in first and second. Their speed and reliability were marvelled at by all. In the same year they both participated in the Evelyn Ellis Rally to celebrate the centenary of the first recorded motorcar journey in the British Isles. Robin Loder drove the 1898 prototype AE 174, No. 18 in the Run, and Richard Eastmead drove the 1900 hackney carriage, AE 341, No. 40 in the Run. (Frontispiece)

Clevedon's heritage in the history of the cars was not forgotten and the town held a cavalcade of veteran cars in the summer of 2006 at which both cars attended. Colour Plate C32 shows the prototype car AE 174 in the foreground with the old Stephens Motor Works in the background. It is now a St Peter's Hospice Shop. Julia Elton, great-grand-daughter of Sir Edmund and President of the Clevedon Civic Society, is in the passenger seat, wearing a red hat.

Clevedon Court is now in the care of the National Trust But the present Baronet Sir Charles Elton lives there with his family, as do Julia and her husband James. The prototype Automatic Gas Lighters are still in the family and the house contains a fine collection of *Eltonware* as well as a collection of coloured glassware including much from the now